The Transforming Power of Spiritual Desire

A Collection of Devotional Readings

Darlene Bishop

Legacy Publishers International
Denver, Colorado

The Transforming Power of Spiritual Desire – Devotional

ISBN 1-880809-39-7
ISBN 978-1-880809-39-6

Legacy Publishers International
1301 South Clinton Street
Denver, CO 80247
Phone: 303-283-7480 Fax: 303-283-7536
www.legacypublishersinternational.com

Manuscript prepared by Melissa Killian, Killian Creative, Boulder, Colorado. www.killiancreative.com

Library of Congress Cataloging-in-Publication Data

Bishop, Darlene

2 3 4 5 6 7 8 9 10 11 12 13 14 15 / 13 12 11 10 09 08 07

Table of Contents

INTRODUCTION

The Power of Desire

Therefore I say unto you, What things soever ye desire, when ye pray, believe that ye receive them, and ye shall have them.

Mark 11:24

Desire is a strange thing. When God uses it, it's wonderful. But when the devil takes hold of it, the results are inevitably tragic. We need strong desires in our lives, but we need to make sure what the source of those desires is and who is controlling them.

One morning I was in prayer. I was asking the Lord to help me bring my every thought under subjection to Him. I wanted to have His mind and to think His thoughts, so that His river could flow out through me more forcefully. As I prayed, the Lord showed me that when the devil gives us a thought, and that thought becomes a desire within us, we're in trouble. But when God gives us a thought, and that thought becomes a desire within us, then the devil's in trouble. **When**

the Lord puts something into our spirit, it takes hold of us and becomes a powerful force that can transform our lives for good. More of us need God-inspired desire.

The strength of our spiritual desire determines not only our present lot in life, but also our future destiny. Desire underlies our effectiveness in prayer, our intensity in worship, and the depth of our personal relationship with God. Desire dictates the enthusiasm with which we take hold of each day and the expectation with which we embrace the future.

Desire is a powerful and energizing force similar to other natural forces such as water, electricity, or fire. It can bring life and hope if directed and channeled for good, or it can destroy and lay waste if not properly harnessed. The direction and intensity of our desire is life changing—world changing for that matter. Your desire determines your destiny—more importantly, without desire nothing worthwhile could be accomplished in God.

It's time to let God put a new burning zeal within our spirits to be all that He has called us to be and to do all that He has called us to do. If revival is to come to the church as a whole, many things have to change. Our temples must be cleansed. There must come a return of the separation God calls for between His people and the world, and men and women of God must again have Him as their source of all things. All of this requires desire on our part.

It is my prayer that this devotional would be a daily tool for you to stir up and refocus your desires so that you don't miss the divine destiny God has called you to—and so that you would become the powerful force for God's kingdom you were created to be. Never underestimate the power of your desire.

Daily we pray: *Father, make me mindful of those special desires You have birthed in me for such a time as this. Help me Lord to be faithful in zealously pursuing those hidden passions You created just for me to delight in and bring forth as a unique blessing to Your Kingdom. I praise You today knowing you are completing the good work You have begun in me. Amen.*

I have learned that in order to bring about change, you must not be afraid to take the first step. We will fail when we fail to try. Each and every one of us can make a difference.

Rosa Parks

There is an inseparable link between your desire and your destiny.

x

ONE

Nothing Is Accomplished Without Desire

Caleb said unto her, What wilt thou? And she said unto him, Give me a blessing: for thou hast given me a south land; give me also springs of water. And Caleb gave her the upper springs and the nether springs.

Judges 1:14,15

As a wedding gift, Caleb gave his daughter, Achsah, some land described in the Bible as *"a south land."* Strangely, she wasn't satisfied with this gift. Apparently the land in question was dry, for the daughter now asked Caleb to give her some source of water, some *"springs"* so that she could irrigate the land. Achsah was wise enough to know that dry land would not produce a suitable livelihood for her family. "Daddy," she urged. "Thank you for the land, but there's something else I need. Could you give me some springs to water it?"

This request didn't anger Caleb in the least. He loved his daughter and wanted her to have the best of everything. If she needed a spring, he wanted her to have a spring. His response was to give her even more than she had requested. He gave her two groups of springs: *"the upper springs and the nether springs."*

That's just like our God. He always gives us more than we request, to show us His great love. But does this story have anything to do with us today in the twenty-first century? Oh, it has everything to do with us. Nothing is accomplished in God's kingdom without desire. **Desire is the very bedrock of our faith. Without a "want to" you will never do anything in the Spirit realm.**

In the story, everyone had a desire. Caleb wanted the place known as Debir; Othniel wanted Achsah as his wife; and Achsah wanted some springs to water her land and make it fruitful. In the end, everyone got what they wanted. That's how powerful a force desire is.

Father God, forgive me for neglecting to seek You, as perhaps I should have, regarding certain desires You have placed in my heart. I ask You today to resurrect those desires and show me how I can more faithfully pursue any desires that have laid dormant. Show me what steps I might take to bring them to pass, the questions I should be asking and the people I should be inquiring of. Thank You for Your mercy and faithfulness as I seek to fulfill all You have placed in my heart for such a time as this. Amen.

Then Queen Esther answered, "If I have found favor with you, O King, and if it pleases your majesty, grant me my life–this is my petition. And spare my people–this is my request."

Esther 7:3 NIV

TWO

Desire Is a Force to Be Reckoned With

Thou openest thine hand, and satisfiest the desire of every living thing.

Psalm 145:16

W*ebster's Dictionary* defines desire in this way: "A wish or longing; a request or petition; the object of longing" **Desire is not just an inclination to want;** it's a force to be reckoned with. **It is a boiling, passionate zeal.** It's not just a whimsical fancy, as some might imagine; it's an overwhelming compulsion.

Whatever we desire we can have. Still, many of us dare to go to the house of God without desire, and once there, we dare to utter prayers that are little more than momentary wishes, flashes in the mind. Usually, before we have left the church building, we've already forgotten what we prayed about that day. Whatever it was, it didn't captivate our souls.

This current generation doesn't seem to be very desirous of the things of God. Perhaps it's because their desire has been turned to the flesh. This, of course, is dangerous. Paul wrote to the Ephesians:

> *Among whom also we all had our conversation in times past in the lusts of our flesh, fulfilling the desires of the flesh and of the mind; and were by nature the children of wrath, even as others.*
>
> Ephesians 2:3

All of us were guilty of feeding the desires of the flesh before we came to know Christ. But after we are already His, there are things that clearly should not be cultivated and nurtured in our lives. They are *"desires of the flesh and of the mind,"* and fulfilling them will cause us to lose many of the spiritual battles we face. How can we be victorious in the things of the Spirit if we're too busy fulfilling the desires of the flesh? The reason many get old before their time is that they have lost their spiritual desire. Once this happens, you might as well start picking out your tombstone. If you have no more desire, you've lost everything. But as long as you have the Spirit of God, God's desires are within you. Stir up the desires God has placed in your heart by delighting again and again in Him.

What is your burning desire? What do you seek after with fervent, boiling zeal? How can you more consistently nurture your God-given passions?

Lord, help me to stay passionate for those desires You've placed in my heart. Help me to continue pursuing them with singleness of heart and not grow weary or doubtful. Thank You for Your enthusiasm at work in me! An ember of Your consuming fire ablaze in my heart. Amen.

Desire is one of the main forces driving a person's life. How a person expresses his desires, follows them, ignores them, reacts to their satisfaction or lack of fulfillment is a measure of a person's character. The power of desire is so tremendous it is hard to ignore.

Susan Minot

THREE

Prayer Must Be Rooted in Desire

Thou hast given him his heart's desire, and hast not withholden the request of his lips.

Psalm 21:2

One of the things most affected by a loss of spiritual desire is our prayer life. It's not enough just to pray. We have to pray out of true desire.

We usually emphasize the need for faith with our prayers, and this is an important element, but desire is clearly just as important. If there's no desire, why pray in the first place? The reason your prayers are not being answered may be the lack of any fervent, boiling, zeal behind them. For instance, if I ask a crowd of Christians how many of them want a spiritual gift to operate in their lives, every hand in the house goes up. But if that's true, why don't they possess the spiritual gifts they desire? Could it be because they don't have a fervent, boiling, zeal for them, a compelling desire that would not let them rest until they had them in place?

Oh, yes, people say, "I'd love to have the gift of healing," but then they're in such a hurry to get out of the service and go somewhere to eat that they don't have time to wait for the prayer around the altar. That speaks louder than their words.

What we call vision is often nothing more than a desire planted in our hearts by the Lord. One of our favorite Bible statements is this:

Where there is no vision, the people perish.

Proverbs 29:18

What sort of vision does this verse speak of? Is this the kind of vision in which you're knocked to the floor and you see a motion picture on the back of your eyelids? No, this reference to *"vision"* means that you have a certain goal, or desire, ever before you. When you have such a vision, you think about it and talk about it constantly, and you pray about it until it becomes a reality. **Revival, or spiritual renewal, often begins with one person's**

vision, one person's spiritual desire. This is a transforming force.

Thank You Father for the courage to desire big things! To envision great works being done for Your Kingdom and the faith to pray them through. Thank You for the hope and expectation we have in You and the power of Your Spirit. Help me Lord not to draw back in doubt and unbelief, but to be bold and purposeful and to run with faith and great desire the race You have set before me. Help me to remember that I can do all things through Christ. Amen.

The Holy Spirit does not come on machinery but on men. He does not anoint plans, but men–men of prayer.

Edward McKendree (E.M.) Bounds

FOUR

To Change Your Situation, Change Your Desire

Sir, I have no man, when the water is troubled, to put me into the pool: but while I am coming, another steppeth down before me.

John 5:7

One day Jesus passed by the Pool of Bethesda. He saw the man who had been sitting in the same place for so long, and He asked him a rather amazing question:

Wilt thou be made whole?

John 5:6

It seems like a ridiculous question to ask a person who's been lying at the same place for many years in hopes of being healed, but when we examine the context, the question was not ridiculous at all. The crippled man had somehow lost his expectation, and his desire had dwindled. Unless he could change his desire, his situation wouldn't change either.

He had been coming to the Pool of Bethesda for so long that he forgot why he had come in the first place. His visit there had become a way of life rather than a portal into a new one. **Jesus was there to remind him of his purpose and destiny, to stir up his desire once again.**

What this man experienced in the physical is so common among Christians today. When we're newly saved, we go to church with great desire and expectation. We want to offer our special gifts and be of service. But sometimes it seems that God is using everybody else but us, so we decide to just sit down for a while and be a "normal" church member.

When this happens, it represents a loss of desire on our part, and what follows is a tragedy. All too soon, our youth passes, and we suddenly find ourselves much older, but still we've not done anything of substance for the Lord. When Jesus asked the man this question, the man had an answer, and most of us would think it was a good one: *Sir, I have no man, when the water is troubled, to put me into the pool.* People had failed him, so he had given up the hope of ever receiving his miracle.

Father God, help me not to draw back from Your highest purpose for me. Help me to boldly take hold of all You have prepared for me to accomplish in You. Help me to stir up the gifts You have placed in me even as the angel stirred up the waters – and help me to walk in them fully, not to be idle or complacent, but to rise to every challenge by faith. Thank You Lord for Your spirit of power, love, and a sound mind at work in me. Amen.

When God works in us, the will, being changed and sweetly breathed upon by the Spirit of God, desire and acts, not from compulsion, but responsively.

Martin Luther

FIVE

Desire Will Rejuvenate You

The desire accomplished is sweet to the soul.

Proverbs 13:19

The loss of hope and the loss of spiritual desire are very much the same thing. Losing either will give the same result. Without desire, we are without hope, and without hope, we are truly lost and left to a life of misery and despair. What could be worse? The loss of hope is always a terrible thing. The writer of the Proverbs said:

Hope deferred maketh the heart sick.

Proverbs 13:12

Anytime you lose hope, your heart becomes sick. Yet there is another part to this verse, and it's very powerful. It says:

But when the desire cometh, it is a tree of life.

Proverbs 13:12

This refers to the tree of life that was situated in the midst of the garden of Eden and represented everything mankind needed to live an abundant life. That's how powerful desire is. Hope that is deferred makes you sick, but desire will rejuvenate you. It will give you a reason to jump out of bed every morning, a reason to comb your hair, get dressed, and get out of the house to see what the day holds for you.

Thank God for that. There are far too many people who are confined to their homes these days, and their life consists of soap operas and junk magazines. **How good it is to be out and about for the kingdom of God! How good it is to feel useful in this world! How good it is to have destiny and purpose!**

After Proverbs 13 speaks of *"hope deferred"* making the soul sick and desire providing *"a tree of life,"* it goes on to make another wonderful statement about the importance of desire:

The desire accomplished is sweet to the soul.

Proverbs 13:19

The antidote for hopelessness is desire! The power of a small seed of desire planted and cultivated in the heart has exponential affects on the health and vitality of the soul. What more needs to be said? It's time to stir up our spiritual desire.

Thank You Lord for Your desires at work in me causing me to will *and to* do *Your good pleasure. Thank You for ordering my steps and helping me to be more mindful of Your presence. Praise You Father for causing Your pleasure to become my pleasure and Your joy to be my strength. Help me to bring You honor and glory even as You continue to fulfill the desires of my heart in Christ. Amen.*

On days when life is difficult and I feel overwhelmed, as I do fairly often, it helps to remember in my prayers that all God requires of me is to trust Him and be His friend. I find I can do that.

Bruce Larson

SIX

Desire Always Finds a Way

Behold, men brought a paralyzed man on a cot, and they sought to bring him in to lay before Him. Not finding a way to bring him in because of the multitude, they went up to the housetop, and let him down through the tiles with his cot into the midst before Jesus. Seeing their faith, he said to him, "Man, your sins are forgiven you."

Luke 5:18-25 WEB

One day Jesus was preaching in a house in Capernaum, and four men came bearing a litter with a sick friend on it. They had heard it said that everyone whom Jesus touched was healed, and they were determined to get their friend to Him.

But, alas, when they got there, all of the handicapped parking spaces were taken, and the fire marshal had declared the meeting at full capacity and closed the doors. There was no way to get their friend inside.

Most of us would have decided about then that it must not have been God's will to heal the man, but these four men were different. They had a burning desire that would not be denied. They could not give up that easily, and they began looking for some other way to get the task accomplished.

Eventually they decided to take the man up onto the roof and lower him down to Jesus. Where did they get the ladder to get up there and the tools they needed to take the roof apart? We don't know. What we do know is that they did whatever was necessary to get it done. Desire always finds a way.

When you have a desire to do something for God, there are not enough demons in hell to stop you. If God has called you to preach, someone may refuse to recognize your calling and give you an opportunity. But if you have a burning desire to do it anyway, you'll find some place to preach—even if it's on some busy street corner. As the old saying goes, "Where there's a will, there's a way."

Real desire is overwhelming and causes you to say, "I've simply got to have it! I'm going to get it! **And nothing and no one will stop me!"**

Do you still have that kind of spiritual desire? Have you underestimated your ability to move mountains for Jesus? Pray today that the Lord will remind you of His greatest desire for your destiny and give you a burning determination to see it accomplished. You can do all things in Christ who strengthens you—through the knowledge of Him who has called you—for greater is He that is in you than he that is in the world—Christ in you, the hope of glory!

Rich is the person who has a praying friend.

Janice Hughes

SEVEN

Desire Will Turn Your Life Upside Down

And her daughter was made whole from that very hour.

Matthew 15:28

Years ago, when I read the story of the woman of Canaan who approached Jesus, I couldn't understand it. This woman came to the Lord and told Him that her daughter was *"grievously vexed with a devil"* (Matthew 15:22), but His response and that of His disciples was very unusual:

But he answered her not a word. And his disciples came and besought him, saying, Send her away; for she crieth after us.

Matthew 15:23

Why would Jesus ignore a woman who was seeking His help? And why would the disciples try to send her away? That was humiliating. Jesus explained His actions this way:

> *I am not sent but unto the lost sheep of the house of Israel.*
>
> Matthew 15:24

When the woman didn't seem to be dissuaded by this response, Jesus answered her further, making His position very clear:

> *It is not meet to take the children's bread, and to cast it to dogs.*
>
> Matthew 15:26

That was about as harsh as anyone could be, and still this woman was not turned away by Jesus' words. He had first ignored her, and the disciples had tried to send her away. Then He had told her plainly that He was only sent to *"the lost sheep of the house of Israel."* When all of that hadn't worked, He told her that it was not right to take *"the children's bread"* and give it to *"dogs."*

Amazingly, this woman pressed on, and what she said next touched the heart of Jesus:

> *Truth, Lord: yet the dogs eat of the crumbs, which fall from their masters' table.*
>
> Matthew 15:27

With desire like that, who could be stopped? Jesus' next response has amazed men and women in every generation:

> *O woman, great is thy faith: be it unto thee even as thou wilt.*
>
> Matthew 15:28

Because of the intensity of her desire, this woman received what she wanted. **True desire simply will not be denied. It will move the hand of God every time.** It will deliver your children from sin, and it will bring healing to your sick body. It's time to pray for renewed spiritual desire, for having it will surely turn your life upside down.

Father God, help me to turn this world upside down! Help me to more passionately pursue the life changing desires You've put within me. Put in me Your burning zeal to see souls saved, Your desperate desire to see the weak made strong, the broken made whole, the captives made free. Help me to be ever more tenacious in seeking You, Your kingdom, and Your righteousness. Amen.

We need men so possessed by the Spirit of God that God can think His thoughts through our minds, that He can plan His will through our actions, that He can direct His strategy of world evangelization through His Church.

Alan Redpath

EIGHT

Desire Produces Results

Blind Bartimaeus, the son of Timaeus, sat by the highway side begging. And when he heard that it was Jesus of Nazareth, he began to cry out, and say, Jesus, thou Son of David, have mercy on me. And many charged him that he should hold his peace: but he cried the more a great deal, Thou Son of David, have mercy on me.

Mark 10:46,47

A blind man named Bartimaeus was sitting by the roadside begging one day when he heard the approach of many people. He asked someone what was going on, and they told him that Jesus of Nazareth was passing that way. When Bartimaeus heard this news, he began to cry out: *Jesus, thou Son of David, have mercy on me!*

Many people tried to silence Bartimaeus that day, but he refused to be silenced. Instead, he cried out even louder. Eventually, Jesus couldn't help but notice this persistent and determined man. "Bring that man who has such great desire," He must have said. "I cannot pass by without healing him." I can somehow picture Bartimaeus that day, getting up and stumbling his way through the crowd. People pushed him aside, but that didn't stop him. They tried to hush him up, but that didn't stop him. He knew that he somehow needed to get Jesus' attention if he was to receive his miracle, and he desperately wanted to be healed. That desire would not allow him to give way to any hindrance. He must persist, and he did.

It's interesting to note that Bartimaeus got Jesus' attention by making enough noise. Yet the trend in our modern churches is for all of us to maintain silence in the services. How can this be right? When people go to a ball game, they scream and jump for their favorite team to win. May God help us to have the same desire for spiritual things as we have for the carnal.

When Bartimaeus, a man who had never seen the light of day stood before Jesus, it took only a simple touch from the Master's hand to bring light flooding into his eyes. Imagine it! The very first thing Bartimaeus saw was the incarnate Son of

God standing in front of him. **His desire had produced the longed-for result and much more**, and from that day onward, Bartimaeus followed Jesus.

All of us could use more of this boiling zeal that comes with real spiritual desire.

What desires have you been waiting to see fulfilled? What results have you been hoping and praying for? Do you have a need that is not being met, and you've been wondering how long until God will hear you and act on your behalf? There are times to patiently wait, and times to be in hot pursuit. What might you do to be more like blind Bartimaeus? Pray about what the Lord would require of you today.

Bear up the hands that hang down, by faith and prayer; support the tottering knees. Have you any days of fasting and prayer? Storm the throne of grace and persevere therein, and mercy will come down.

John Wesley

NINE

Renew Your Desire

Delight thyself also in the Lord; and he shall give thee the desires of thine heart. Commit thy way unto the Lord; trust also in him; and he shall bring it to pass.

Psalm 37:4,5

A wonderful biblical example of spiritual desire and what it can accomplish is the story of Nehemiah. This man was a slave captured in Israel and taken to Persia. There, he rose in importance and became a trusted servant of the king. In this capacity, he was doing well—until one day his world was turned upside down.

When someone told Nehemiah that the holy city of Jerusalem had been looted and burned and that its once regal walls and gates now lay in ruins, the news so disturbed him that he could no longer perform his duties in a proper way. He asked the king for a leave of absence so that he could go back home and try to rebuild the city. Amazingly, this request was granted.

When Nehemiah arrived in Jerusalem, he found the situation worse than he imagined. Not only was the once great city decimated, it was surrounded by enemies. He gathered the Jewish people in and around the city and told them his plan to rebuild. If they were willing to join him in this task, they would have to work with their trowels in one hand and their weapons in the other. They could do it, he assured them.

Then an astonishing thing happened. Despite their limitations, these people (none of them masons or carpenters by trade) were able to do the needed work in just fifty-two days. **Nehemiah's desire built walls and gates and restored the city for the people of Jerusalem. And that's what renewed spiritual desire will do for you too.**

The Lord is committed to giving you the desires of your heart, but He also requires something of you. *"Delight thyself in the Lord."* That's your part of the bargain, and it indicates to the Lord the level of your spiritual desire.

Delight yourself in the Lord so that you can become intimately familiar with His heart, that your heart will be shaped to fit into His perfectly, that you might become of one heart and mind in Christ. Ask God to unite your heart to His and keep it connected by delighting in His presence continually.

With the light of your presence and warmth of your love, Lord, furnish my heart and make it your home.

B.J. Hoff

TEN

Sanctify Your Desire

Walk in the Spirit, and ye shall not fulfill the lust of the flesh. For the flesh lusteth against the Spirit, and the Spirit against the flesh: and these are contrary the one to the other: so that ye cannot do the things that ye would.

Galatians 5:16,17

Othniel wanted a wife, and that desire prompted him to fight giants and overrun a city. And we, too, can have what we want in God—if we really want it badly enough and go after it with fiery zeal. But, Satan, too, utilizes desire. If he can make us Christians want something that we shouldn't have bad enough, he knows that we'll do anything to get it—even risk alienating ourselves from God. Such an overpowering desire is known in scripture as *"the lust of the flesh."*

The sad thing is that most Christians know that the thing they're pursuing will take them straight to hell, but they become so obsessed with it that they're sure they just can't live without it. The results of such a pursuit are always very devastating.

One of King David's sons, Amnon, became obsessed with his half-sister Tamar. He was so sick with desire for her that it drove him to rape her. Then, when the evil deed was done, he despised Tamar so much that he wanted her out of his sight immediately. Do you see how Satan works? He convinces you that you need something so badly that you just can't live without it, and then, once you have it, you're sick about it. It didn't bring you the joy you thought it would. The result was even sadder for Amnon. His mistake cost him his life, and that is the price Satan wants to make you pay for sin as well. As Jesus said to Peter:

> *Simon, Simon, behold, Satan hath desired to have you, that he may sift you as wheat.*
>
> Luke 22:31

Satan wants you so badly that he's willing to do most anything to get you. **Put yourself firmly on the side of God's desire.**

Are there desires in your own life that you know are not of God—that are potentially dangerous to your destiny? Pray the Lord exposes any desires that are holding you back, that the Holy Spirit works in your heart to stir you only to pursue desires that are of God, and that those desires are fulfilled through you for His glory.

My great concern is not whether God is on our side. My great concern is to be on God's side.

Abraham Lincoln

ELEVEN

Stir the Fire of Your Desire

One thing have I desired of the Lord, that will I seek after; that I may dwell in the house of the Lord all the days of my life, to behold the beauty of the Lord, and to inquire in his temple.

Psalm 27:4

What we desire is what we seek after, and because David's desire was toward God, he became *"a man after his own heart"* (1 Samuel 13:14). My mamma always said that you can talk to somebody for ten minutes and know where their heart is. It doesn't take long.

If we are to get anything from God, we first must have a spiritual desire, and if we are to continue being blessed by God, we must not lose that spiritual desire. Fight to maintain it fresh and strong.

I notice the young men and women who gather on the front rows of our churches. They're so fervent that they never miss a service, and they love God so much that they jump higher than anyone else during the worship times. But if they're not careful, they'll gradually lose that fervency.

Such a desire must be cultivated and must lead to our doing something for God and His kingdom. **God puts a desire within you, and if you don't do something with it, it will die.** And when your desire dies, your spirituality will die with it.

I see it all the time. People get saved, and they have a zeal to do something great for God. Then, before long, I see them sitting calmly and quietly like everyone else, satisfied to go though the motions without any real excitement or determination. Oh, please don't lose the fire of your spiritual desire. Keep it ever burning bright, and your future will be just as bright.

Almighty God, You are great and greatly to be praised! Thank You for Your goodness and mercy toward us. Thank You for Your Spirit that comforts us and guides us into all Truth. Thank You for Your Word in our hearts, Your Name on our lips, and Your Presence ever with us. We seek You with all our hearts, and love You with all our strength. You are worthy of all honor and glory, and nothing on this earth compares to You!

Spirit-filled souls are ablaze for God. They love with a love that glows. They serve with a faith that kindles. They serve with a devotion that consumes. They hate sin with fierceness that burns. They rejoice with a joy that radiates. Love is perfected in the fire of God.

Samuel Chadwick

TWELVE

God Rewards Desire

But without faith it is impossible to please him: for he that cometh to God must believe that he is, and that he is a rewarder of them that diligently seek him.

Hebrews 11:6

What does it mean to diligently seek God? It means that we crave to investigate more about Him. We long to search out His hidden parts. We long to learn to worship Him in new ways. We want what He wants for us. Our God rewards such desire. The Scriptures declare:

Ask, and it shall be given you; seek, and ye shall find; knock, and it shall be opened unto you: for every one that asketh receiveth; and he that seeketh findeth: and to him that knocketh it shall be opened.

Matthew 7:7,8

Blessed are they that keep his testimonies, and that seek him with the whole heart.

Psalm 119:2

The Lord searcheth all hearts, and understandeth all the imaginations of the thoughts: if thou seek him, he will be found of thee.

1 Chronicles 28:9

God rewards diligence and not slothfulness. Those who do only what is required of them on their job should not be looking for either a raise or a promotion. Far too many people say, "That's not part of my job description." That's okay, but let's see what happens when promotion time comes. Promotion comes to us only when we have become overqualified for our current position.

Some people want to do public ministry, but they don't do a good job with the first simple tasks assigned to them. If you can't be faithful in the nursery, how can you qualify to head up some critical ministry of the church? When you're overqualified for the spot you now occupy, then God will promote you to another division of His kingdom. When you become overqualified for your current position, you also become dissatisfied and want to move on. **Desire moves you up the ladder.**

Two of the first things we are taught as Christians is to submit ourselves to God so that He might exalt us in due time—and that promotion comes from the Lord. We have heard the famous words of Isaiah 57:15, "I dwell in the high and holy place, with him also that is of a contrite and humble spirit, to revive the spirit of the humble, and to revive the heart of the contrite ones." Thank You Lord for creating a clean and upright heart in me, that I might be a minister of Your grace.

Nothing disciplines the inordinate desires of the flesh like service, and nothing transforms the desires of the flesh like serving in hiddenness. The flesh whines against service but it screams against hidden service. It strains and pulls for honor and recognition.

Richard Foster

THIRTEEN

Desire Keeps You Focused

Desire spiritual gifts.

1 Corinthians 14:1

If you don't have spiritual gifts, it may be because you haven't desired them enough. When we go to God, we don't seem to be absolutely sure of what we want from Him. One day it's one thing, and the next day it's something else entirely. But desire keeps us focused. It causes us to say, "I'm not leaving here until I get that. I want that, and I won't stop until it's mine."

We go to bed thinking about it, we wake up thinking about it, and we go through the day thinking about it. We might be driving a car and doing a good job of it, but at the same time, the desire on the inside of us is saying, "I want more of God."

When we truly hunger for God, we get very specific about our desire. In this way, our desire actually determines our destiny, for God responds to hungry people:

Blessed are they which do hunger and thirst after righteousness: for they shall be filled.

Matthew 5:6

This is one of God's inviolable laws. The hunger of a man's soul must be satisfied. That's His commitment. He fills all those who recognize that they have a need. Those who are not hungry need not apply.

David knew this secret. He said:

As the hart panteth after the water brooks, so panteth my soul after thee, O God. My soul thirsteth for God, for the living God.

Psalm 42:1,2

This is the same panting desire of which the writer of Hebrews speaks in Hebrews 11:6. **To diligently seek God carries the meaning of experiencing a passion that causes you to breathe hard.**

David was panting after God. He simply had to have Him. There was nothing that he wanted more in life. He was king over Israel, so he had plenty of resources at his disposal. He had all the women he could ever want, and yet there was something that drove him forward. This one thing dominated his thinking and motivated his every word and action. He desperately wanted more of God.

What dominates your thinking? What dominates your desire? Are you desperate for more of God? What commands your focus, your thoughts, your concerns? Purpose today to keep God at the center of your thought-life—to be God-minded. "Be being continually filled with the Spirit, speaking out in psalms and spiritual songs, making melody in your heart unto the Lord, giving thanks always for all things unto God the Father in the name of our Lord Jesus Christ." (Ephesians 5:17-20)

Give me the love that leads the way, / The faith that nothing can dismay, / The hope no disappointments tire, / The passion that will burn like fire, / Let me not sink to be a clod: / Make me Thy fuel, Flame of God.

Amy Carmichael

FOURTEEN

Necessity: The Invention of Desire

I would rather be a doorkeeper in the house of my God than dwell in the tents of wickedness. For the Lord God is a sun and shield; The Lord will give grace and glory; No good thing will He withhold from those who walk uprightly. O Lord of hosts, blessed is the man who trusts in You!

Psalm 84:10-12 TMB

God never does the unnecessary. He gives sight to the blind, not to those who can already see. He heals the sick, not those who are healthy. He lifts up the fallen, not those who are still standing. And, in this same way, He raises up the "nobodies" of this world, not those who are already "somebodies."

When Jesus was on the earth, He went to the needy. And God still meets us at the point of our need, not at the point of our preferences. This is because need produces desire.

David had an all-consuming desire for God, and it was that desire that elevated him to the throne of Israel. God knew that David wasn't after position or power. His all-consuming desire was not to be wealthy, to have a crown on his head, or to hear people calling him "King." No, David would have been satisfied to be a doorkeeper in God's house.

David was intent on seeking after God, and what we seek is what we get. If what you desire is illicit drugs, then you'll become a drug addict. If you desire alcohol, you'll become an alcoholic. If your desire is a perverted sexual lust, then you'll eventually have a perverted, lusting demon in you.

What is your greatest desire? Some would actually say a better golf game, to star in the NBA, or to become the CEO of a large company. What is it that you think about when you go to bed at night? What fills your thoughts each new day? Well, whatever it is, that's what you'll become, for your desire ultimately determines your destiny.

God is made strong in weakness, and is most glorified in seemingly ordinary things. God lifts up the humble. He looks for faithfulness in the details of life and seeks to be known in that which is most easily overlooked. Though our God is majestic, we often see Him most glorified in the mundane. It seems that faithfulness is most exemplified by what we do and who we are in the unsung, secret moments of our lives.

One of the most important discoveries I have ever made is this truth: God is most glorified in me when I am most satisfied in him. This is the motor that drives my ministry as a pastor. It affects everything I do.

John Piper

FIFTEEN

The Desire of First Love

I have somewhat against thee, because thou hast left thy first love.

Revelation 2:4

When people first get saved, they experience what the Bible calls their "first love." **I am convinced that our "first love" represents God's perfect will for our lives.** He places certain desires in us, and we hunger for those specific things. This changes everything about our lives.

"First love" is contagious. You're excited, and you want to tell everyone about it. You want to go to church every time the doors are open. You just can't get enough of the Word of God. On your lunch hour, you sit and read the Bible or some good Christian book. Your appetite for God seems endless.

You don't just go to church on Sundays; you can hardly wait for Wednesday night to come. I have people call me to ask, "Do you know anyone who's having church on Mondays? Wednesday is too long for me to wait." That's what first love will do for you. It puts within you a seemingly inexhaustible desire for more of God.

"First love" also gives you a desire to work for God. After I got saved, all I wanted to do was preach. Every time I saw someone preaching, I thought, "I want to preach just like that, if God would just give me sermons to deliver." I was so serious about this that I actually began outlining sermons that I hoped to someday deliver.

As it turned out, I wasn't able to go into ministry right away because Lawrence and I got married and had children, and it took all of my efforts to raise them. For a while, it seemed that my dream of preaching would never come true, but God hadn't forgotten it—and I hadn't forgotten it either.

The reason I eventually did begin preaching was that the desire to preach had never left me. God puts a desire in your heart, as part of your first love. In that moment, your desire and His desire become one, and that union of desire will eventually bring forth the intended fruit—if you determine never to lose your "first love." You actually become pregnant with desire, and nothing can satisfy you until you've given birth to that desire.

Remember how it felt when you first tasted God's love and gave your heart to him? How did those feelings dictate your desires? What were the desires that consumed you when you first came to know the Lord? Lay hold of those "first desires"—what you wanted most when you came to the knowledge of the Truth. Revive that anticipation you first felt and let it inform how you approach life's decisions now—purpose to give into your first love.

God's commands are designed to guide you to life's very best. You will not obey Him, if you do not believe Him and trust Him. You cannot believe Him if you do not love Him. You cannot love Him unless you know Him.

Henry Blackaby

SIXTEEN

God's Holy Desire for You

And the Lord said, Simon, Simon, behold, Satan hath desired to have you, that he may sift you as wheat: but I have prayed for thee, that thy faith fail not: and when thou art converted, strengthen thy brethren.

Luke 22:31,32

Just as God has a holy desire for each of us, Satan has an evil desire for each of us. He desired to do Peter damage because he knew how much good Peter could do for the kingdom of God. The original language of the above passage gives the sense that Satan demanded permission to have Peter, but God refused.

This phrase *"when thou art converted,"* in the original Greek, conveys the meaning, "when you retrace your steps." It was only after Peter had retraced his steps that he would be personally convinced of the truth, and only then could he strengthen his brothers. At the moment this was spoken, he wasn't sure, but after Jesus died and then resurrected, he would retrace his steps, see that everything Jesus said was true, and that He was the Son of God. Then he would be ready to convert others.

It's time that each of us retrace our steps. Go back and take another look, and in the process, let spiritual desire be rekindled.

Didn't God heal you once or more than once? Didn't He miraculously supply your needs on several occasions or even many occasions? Didn't He bring you out of trouble? Well, if He did that once, can He not do it again? After all, He's *"the same yesterday, and to day, and for ever"* (Hebrews 13:8). He said:

> *For I am the Lord, I change not.*
>
> Malachi 3:6

Just as He did for Peter, **God will stand in the gap and make up the hedge for you. He will fight to see that you keep your desire**. But it's up to you to see that you continue to seek Him.

You should because He's never failed you yet. It is as you persevere in Him that your desire will bring forth your destiny.

Thank You Father God for Your everlasting love and steadfast faithfulness to me. You have always come through, always been there, and I will ever be watchful over me as I pursue You with my whole heart. Help my faith not to fail as I seek to do Your will. Thank You Holy Spirit for making God's desires my desires and helping me not to lose heart. Lord, You alone are my hope and inspiration and only in You can I hope to accomplish anything worthwhile. I love and trust You with my whole heart!

How would your day unfold if you believed that God wants your borders expanded at all times with every person and if you were confident that God's powerful hand was directing you?

Bruce Wilkinson

SEVENTEEN

Exercise Godly Desire

A prudent man foreseeth the evil, and hideth himself: but the simple pass on, and are punished.

Proverbs 22:3

Prudent people prepare for danger, but the simple just plunge on into it and have to suffer the consequences. One prudent step to be taken before reaching for the forbidden fruit might be to take a long and hard look at what has happened to those who have given in to such temptation.

I don't understand it completely, but there's something hypnotic and intoxicating about wickedness. One thing leads to another, and at some point, there seems to be a total disregard for consequences. David said:

The desire of the wicked shall perish.

Psalm 112:10

Too many times, our appetites become our masters, and we become willing to do anything at all to satisfy them. And what is an appetite if not a desire?

Always, when our appetites are for the things of God, Satan comes along with his lies and deceptions and tries to turn us away to other things. If we know the truth in God, we can easily turn him away.

"No, Satan," we can respond. "There was a time when I was tempted by drugs, but no longer. Now I know a satisfaction and excitement that nothing can surpass." Or we can say to him, "No, Satan. There was a time when I was tempted by a good-looking man, but no more. Now I know a Man who truly understands me and stands by me whatever may come." My destiny is too important to let it be damaged or destroyed.

So let the devil push. If you stay true to God, the evil one can't do you any harm. God has promised to hide you under the shadow of His wings.

God has placed eternity in our hearts, so it should not surprise us that earthly things fail to satisfy us. And just **as long as eternity is in our**

hearts, we can stand in the face of temptation and laugh at the enemy.

You can say to Satan, "Take this whole world, but give me Jesus. I'm never turning back. My destiny is too important to allow you to steal it."

God is doing all that He can to help us stand strong in this day, and one of the things He has done is to flood us with His Word. We need it because we just don't have time to "mess up."

Because God has given us so much of His Word, we have no excuse. Just say no to temptation, and the more you resist, the stronger you'll become. It's a lot like a good workout with weight-training equipment. The greater the resistance, the stronger you become. And the stronger you become, the more likely you are to find your true destiny in God.

If I find in myself a desire which no experience in this world can satisfy, the most probable explanation is that I was made for another world.

C.S. Lewis

EIGHTEEN

Let God Restore Your Desire

The gifts and calling of God are without repentance.

Romans 11:29

What is your desire today? Have you let those desires of *"first love"* die within you? Have you aborted the dream before it had a chance to come to life? Have you had a spiritual miscarriage?

God hasn't changed His mind about you, and His gifts are still available to you. Like the daughter of Jairus, they may be sleeping, but they can easily and quickly come to life again.

Just speak to that gift, and let it be reborn. Let God restore to you a desire for Him and the things of His kingdom, a desire to bring others to

His feet, a desire to witness, a desire to be all that God has intended you to be.

Maybe your desire has totally died. You still go to church, but only out of obligation. There's no hunger in you for the things of God. You have no desire to attend prayer meetings. You no longer have a place where you get alone with God and just bask in His presence. When you walk outside in your yard or around the neighborhood, you no longer marvel at His glory and let His great creation inspire you to worship. Let God turn that around for you.

Your desire may be taking you down the road to destruction. Have you begun to desire the things of this world? Do you long to go back to what used to excite you: drugs, alcohol, or some sexual perversion? You can't afford to go that route.

If the fire has grown cold in you, come back to God. Tell Him, "I desire You, Lord, more than anything. I give You all my hopes and dreams. Have Your way in my life today." He will not disappoint you. He will rekindle your love for Him and set your soul on fire afresh and anew. Don't delay another day, for your desire will determine your destiny.

If you need to, get to an altar of prayer. If you can't do that, make an altar there where you are. Say, "Father, rekindle my desire because I'm not where I want to be. I want to go somewhere in You and do something great for You." God will honor your prayer if it is heartfelt. Make this your supplication today—that the Spirit of God would soften your heart and cause a deep hunger for more of Him. Let your heart cry be for a deeper fellowship, greater intimacy, and an ever-present yearning for His Presence.

Give me one hundred preachers who fear nothing but sin and desire nothing but God, and I care not whether they be clergymen or laymen, they alone will shake the gates of hell and set up the kingdom of heaven upon earth.

John Wesley

NINETEEN

Pregnant with Desire

Before she travailed, she brought forth; before her pain came, she was delivered of a man-child. Who hath heard such a thing? who hath seen such things? Shall the earth be made to bring forth in one day? or shall a nation be born at once? for as soon as Zion travailed, she brought forth her children.

Isaiah 66:6,7

God has a desire for your life, and, as we have seen, when His desire becomes your desire, a unity of desire is formed that is not easily broken. You have formed a holy union with the God of the universe, and in the process, you've actually become pregnant with His desire. That changes everything.

If you've ever experienced pregnancy, you know exactly what I'm talking about. Everything you do now revolves around the fact that you have a life growing inside of you. You can't go the same places and do the same things as before. You can't even eat the same things. Life is no longer about you; it's about the life growing inside of you.

Personally, my life is no longer about satisfying the whims of Darlene Bishop; it's about the gift and calling of God that's upon me. Because of that, I can't live like the average person does or do the things they do. And I don't want to. I have a special gift from God, a special calling, and with that special calling comes a special responsibility. I have something to deliver to God's people, and I must deliver it.

When any woman becomes pregnant in the natural, her whole life changes. With every decision she makes, she must now take into consideration the fact that she's pregnant. She goes to bed thinking about it and wakes up the next day thinking about it. Because of this, she does everything necessary to protect that life and to prepare to bring it forth.

It's the same when you become pregnant with godly desire. Every time you go to church, you feel something leap within you. And there are many things you will no longer consider doing. **Things change in your life when you become pregnant with God's desires**, and you don't resent the changes. You're excited about the new life inside of you and willing to make whatever sacrifice is necessary to protect it.

Is there life growing in you? Are you pregnant with God's desires? Maybe you don't feel pregnant because the desire you carry inside hasn't grown much lately. Feed the life growing in you with an abundance of Word and prayer. Determine to carry it to term. Protect that special desire planted in your heart by guarding your thoughts, actions, and words—and pray without ceasing!

Pray often, for prayer is a shield to the soul, a sacrifice to God, and a scourge for Satan.

John Bunyan

TWENTY

God Will Honor Your Desire

Pray without ceasing. In every thing give thanks: for this is the will of God in Christ Jesus concerning you.

1 Thessalonians 5:17,18

When you have a burning God-inspired desire, it becomes the focal point of every prayer meeting. Every time you meet with God, you can hardly wait to get around to asking Him about it. You pray for other things, for the preacher and his or her family, for the nations and for the people of Israel. But, all the while, you're chomping at the bit to talk to God about the seed He has planted within you.

You come to recognize that whenever you're able to pray about your desire, a strange satisfaction comes over you. It seems that the more you pray about it, the more pregnant you become. And the more pregnant you become, the sooner you can hold that baby in your arms. **Prayer is the midwife that will help to bring forth your desire.**

Many have aborted the plan that God has for them because they've been unwilling to pay the price in prayer. Many women get abortions these days for no other reason than the fact that they're selfish. They're not ready to give themselves over to such great responsibility.

Many think they want to be in Christian ministry ... until they discover that Christian ministry requires a whole lot more than just holding a microphone in your hand. In fact, it requires a complete surrender of every aspect of your life to God.

But I have good news. If you have miscarried and the seed of godly desire no longer burns within your soul, God wants to plant a new seed in your womb. Let Him impregnate you with desire afresh today. Let the desire that died inside of you leap back to life. He can do that so easily and quickly.

The desire God now plants in you may be to become a Sunday school teacher. It may be a desire to prophesy or to lay hands on the sick and see them recover. Get ready for your particular God-inspired desire to spring to life in your innermost being. When you are willing to carry His life, God honors your desire.

Oh Lord Jesus, how sweet is Your Name! I cry out to You today and worship Your Beauty—Your Holiness. There is none like You, and no one else on this earth can touch my heart like You do. Touch my heart today, Lord. Like David pleaded in the Psalms of old, "Create in me a clean heart!" Create in me a fresh desire born of Your love, beauty, and holiness at work in me today. You are my hope and my inspiration; only in You will I find completion.

God will manifest himself in direct proportion to our passion for Him.

Jim Cymbala

TWENTY-ONE

Prevailing Through Travailing

For we know that the whole creation groaneth and travaileth in pain together until now.

Romans 8:22

In the Word of God, travail is always connected with grief, pain, and sorrow, and that's no fun. Many have aborted the plan that God has for them because they've been unwilling to pay the price in prayer. And yet **birth doesn't happen without travail**.

I remember vividly the details of the birth of my youngest daughter, Julie. When I got to the hospital, I was given a shot of something that was intended to relax me. In reality, it sedated me.

"This will relax you, Mrs. Bishop," a nurse said. The next thing I knew someone was slapping my face, trying to get me awake. They were saying, "Wake up, Mrs. Bishop, wake up! Your baby's ready to be born, and you've got to bear down and push. If you don't bear down and push, this baby's life will be in jeopardy."

Travail requires a bearing down and a pushing forth, but I was still so sedated that it was hard for me to respond. I heard what they were saying to me, but I couldn't seem to muster the strength to do anything about it.

I would make a noise and grunt like I was pushing, but I wasn't awake enough to really push. It was all lip service. I was like those who have "a form of godliness, but deny the power thereof" (2 Timothy 3:5). They tried slapping me several more times, to get me to cooperate with them, but still they had to use forceps to bring Julie out. I had been so sedated that I wasn't able to push as I should have.

Much like the church of today, we have been sedated by teachings that say we no longer have to pray through a given situation. We can just confess it, speaking the Word, naming and claiming what we want, and it's ours. But I've got news for all who think the Christian life is that easy. Anything and everything you get from God will come by you praying a hole through heaven to get it.

Lord, teach me to pray a hole through heaven! Show me how to travail in order to bring forth life—not only the life You've purposed in me—but the life You've placed in those around me. Help me to see Your life at work in them and to do all I can in the spirit, as well as in the natural, to bring it to pass. Teach me to bear down until I see it come forth!

We are fit for the work of God only when we have wept over it, prayed about it, and then we are enabled by Him to tackle the job that needs to be done.

Alan Redpath

TWENTY-TWO

Desire Brings Forth Life

For ye remember, brethren, our labour and travail: for labouring night and day, because we would not be chargeable unto any of you.

1 Thessalonians 2:9

Travail in the Spirit may be a term that is nearly foreign to most modern American believers, but I'm convinced that it will have to be called back into the church if we're to see the result God has destined for us. Sadly, what we have today is an imitation of real travail. **It's time for us to get serious about travail and bring to birth our destiny.**

One Saturday I was in the church praying, when I felt the spirit of travail come over me. I suddenly felt a great burden for my oldest brother Dale, and I began to weep and call out to God for his soul. Dale was fifty-six years old but still weighed only a hundred and five pounds. He contracted polio shortly after he was born, and, as a result, his body never developed fully. When he eventually began to walk, it was with a very bad limp. Because of Dale's physical limitations, children made fun of him in school, and this led him to develop a very bad attitude toward life.

But that Saturday morning I sensed that something was changing with Dale. I had fallen on my face before God, and as travail came I said, "I will not get up from this place until I feel a change in Dale's life."

That was saying a lot. Dale was now insisting that there was no God and that he hated everyone in our family. He hadn't spoken a word to our mother in five years. "I'm believing for his salvation!" I cried out, and I stayed there in travail for his soul until I felt a release come.

Three days later Dale had an accident on a four-wheeler. He was airlifted to a hospital in Nashville, Tennessee, and someone called to say that they didn't know if he would live or die. When I arrived at the hospital, I was surprised to find him "cussing out" his doctors and nurses. What was happening?

I went back home and committed it all to God. A week later, early one morning, I received a phone call. It was Dale. "Sis," he said, "I just got saved about four o'clock this morning. How can I reach Mamma and Daddy? I've got some things I need to make right with them." I said, "Baby, I already knew it. Three weeks ago, I saw it all, as I was on my face before God in prayer for you." Oh, how we rejoiced together!

That's just how powerful it is to travail in God, and it will always bring your desire to birth. Take hold of those things weighing on your heart in travailing prayer until you feel God lift them from you.

Perhaps if there were more of that intense distress for souls that leads to tears, we should more frequently see the results we desire.

Hudson Taylor

TWENTY-THREE

Giving Birth to Godly Desire

I will turn their mourning into joy.

Jeremiah 31:13

Today we're so lazy and preoccupied with other things that we ask others to do our praying for us. An evangelist friend of mine told me about what happened in one of his recent meetings. A woman came up to him and asked him if he would pray for her husband to be saved. Something came over him, and he answered her in this way: "Sister, have you ever prayed all night long for your husband to be saved?"

"No," she admitted, "I don't suppose I have."

"Have you ever prayed for one solid hour for nothing but the salvation of your husband?" he continued. She thought for a moment and then answered, "Well, I don't suppose I have prayed for him for a solid hour without stopping."

The evangelist then told her, "Why would you ask me to pray for a man I've never met, when he's your husband, and you haven't even prayed for him for one hour? Go sit down."

The woman was highly offended and swore that she would never return to that church as long as that man was there. She thought he was about the meanest man she'd ever met, and she would show him.

Her husband was out of town on a business trip, and when she returned home, she decided that she would pray just for him for a whole hour. With that, she got serious with God, and before long, a spirit of travail came upon her, and she began lamenting and crying out to God.

About three o'clock that next morning, her husband was suddenly awakened with a desire to call his wife. When he couldn't get an answer, he became alarmed. He jumped in his car and drove for four hours until he reached their home. He rushed to get inside and there he found his wife lying on her face, groaning with pain. "What's the matter with you? I drove all night! Why didn't you answer my call early this morning?"

Her answer startled him: "Because I've been praying for you since eleven o'clock last night." He fell on his knees right there and got saved. The next night, she took him with her to the revival meetings.

"This is what I got for praying all night long!" she proudly declared to the evangelist and everyone else present." **That's the power of travailing prayer, and it's because you are giving birth to godly desire.**

There is nothing of greater value than a soul. We endure an uncomfortable pregnancy for nine months followed by hours of travail in order to give birth to a baby, yet we won't inconvenience ourselves, let alone travail, for the eternal salvation of a soul—or an entire nation. Avail yourself to travail for those you love. And then move on to those you don't love, and then to those you don't even know.

If you are having difficulty loving or relating to an individual, take him to God. Bother the Lord with this person. Don't you be bothered with him–leave him at the throne.

Charles R. Swindoll

TWENTY-FOUR

The Dark Depths of Desire

For what knowest thou, O wife, whether thou shalt save thy husband? or how knowest thou, O man, whether thou shall save thy wife?

1 Corinthians 7:16

Many Christian women have thought that they wanted their husbands saved, but that's about all they've done about it. They haven't bothered to take the necessary time and make the necessary effort to pray their loved one through to salvation.

In the church world today, many of us seem to know how to organize, but we no longer know how to agonize. Most of us don't know anything about praying until we're sure that an answer is on its way.

Saying a little prayer is not enough. You have to go to God with true desire and pray out of that desire until your God-inspired petition is fulfilled.

But how can you know when it's time to give birth to your desire? Oh, that's easy. When the pain is more than you can bear, you'll know that it's time. When one of your children is so "messed up" that you don't know what to do next, when you no longer have any answers to life's many problems, when your husband has gone on a rampage and nothing seems to reach him— that's when you'll know that you're ready to give birth.

When it happens, the pain will intensify, and one pain will no more pass than another will be upon you. At this point, you'll know that your desire is about to come forth. When trial follows trial and dilemma follows dilemma, don't despair. Rather, get ready to give birth to something new and wonderful. **Desperation is a wonderful aid to prayer. It makes you get deadly serious before God and helps you give birth to your desire.**

Lord, help me to stand fast in the gap for my loved one. Help me to persevere in faith when it seems all is lost in the natural. When the dark is darkest, I hang on to You Lord—Your promises that my petitions are heard and my deepest longings fulfilled by You. You know my frame and the limits of what I can endure. I thank You that You are refining me, but also that You won't allow me to be overcome. You are faithful. And I thank You that all is working out for good because I love You. To You be all the praise and glory. Amen.

See in the meantime that your faith brings forth obedience, and God in due time will cause it to bring forth peace.

John Owen

TWENTY-FIVE

The Desperate Desire of Deborah

In the days of Shamgar the son of Anath, in the days of Jael, the highways were unoccupied, and the travelers walked through byways. The inhabitants of the villages ceased, they ceased in Israel, until that I Deborah arose, that I arose a mother in Israel.

Judges 5:6,7

Deborah, of Old Testament fame, knew what it was to become desperate before God, and because of that, she became *"a mother in Israel."*

Deborah had a desire, but a desire was not enough. She had to get desperate enough to do something about the current situation. And she did just that. Oh, how we need more mothers in Israel in the church today!

Mothers are more than women who can give birth to a baby. Mothers know how to care for a baby and raise it properly. A real mother knows how to pray because she's discerning. She senses it when her baby's in trouble. Where are all of our mothers in Israel? I'm afraid that they're busy at the spa, the cinema, or the mall.

Real mothers should be teaching our current generation how to raise children themselves. Paul wrote:

> *The aged women likewise, that they be in behaviour as becometh holiness, not false accusers, not given to much wine, teachers of good things; that they may teach the young women to be sober, to love their husbands, to love their children, to be discreet, chaste, keepers at home, good, obedient to their own husbands, that the word of God be not blasphemed.*
>
> Titus 2:3-5

We're still teaching the younger women, but we're only teaching them things like how to fix their hair, how to dress properly, and how to use makeup. It's time that we taught them how to effectively call on Jesus, how to plead His blood over themselves and their family, and how to pray through until victory comes.

It's time that we commit to a new generation the standards that have brought us strength down through the centuries. There was a time here in America when the church set the standards, and the whole country lived by them. Now, it seems, the world sets the standards, and the church lives by them. This ought not to be!

Thank You Lord for Your Word at work in our hearts. Thank You Father for helping us to gird up the loins of our minds, to be circumspect, sober-minded, single-hearted and ever in pursuit of Your will and glory. Thank You for making us mindful of where we are headed and how we can better order our steps and number our days for Your glory. Amen.

For many of us the great danger is not that we will renounce our faith. It is that we will become so distracted and rushed and preoccupied that we will settle for a mediocre version of it.

John Ortberg

TWENTY-SIX

Divine Desire Will Never Expire

For the gifts and calling of God are without repentance.

Romans 11:29

My daddy always planted a garden, and I couldn't help but notice that when he planted squash, its vines took off in all directions. They would pass through the corn, the beans, the potato patch, and the tomato plants, and in time, they would be intertwined with absolutely everything in the garden. Still, the squash plants never changed their nature. Although they were intertwined with everything else, they were still squash, and they still brought forth squash.

This is what I've found to be true also of people who are pregnant with desire. You can place them in a factory, standing alongside a person who's demon possessed, and they can eat their lunch with an atheist, and have a boss who's some kind of pervert, and still they'll never change. Despite the fact that they're forced to listen to every imaginable cursing and perversion all day long, when they walk out of that factory door to go home, they're still a child of God, and they're still pregnant with His desires.

One summer I was preaching in a conference in Canada, and one day I went into a nail salon there to get my nails done. There was a nice-looking young man there, a hairdresser, and he came over to where I was getting my nails done and began to talk to me. He asked if I was from around there and what my plans were for that night. When told him I was preaching, he still persisted in asking me out. When I told him I didn't think my husband would appreciate that he asked if my husband had come with me. I told him he hadn't and that he was welcome to come hear me preach.

"I will," he said. And then he added, "If you'll go out with me afterward."

I had a young lady with me that day, and she was furious with his brazenness. Later, she said to me, "Oh, I got so angry with that young man!

I was rebuking the devil! I was praying for you the whole time."

I smiled. "That was no temptation," I assured her. "I'm pregnant!"

Once you have brought your desire to birth, it's yours, and no one can take it from you. You might, at some point, neglect this new life, and you might even forsake it, but it will still belong to you. **When you get into God's presence, you will know that you can still bring forth your dream**—whatever men may say.

Father God, thank You for keeping Your dream for my life before me, keep reminding me and stirring up Your desire in my heart. Help me to bring it to pass as You see fit, in Your perfect timing. I trust You Lord to complete the good work You have begun in me.

Our entire lives should be about pursuing God and allowing Him to bring about radical Christ-likeness in us.

Bill Nix

TWENTY-SEVEN

Destined for Desire

Let not the wise man glory in his wisdom, neither let the mighty man glory in his might, let not the rich man glory in his riches: But let him that glorieth glory in this, that he understandeth and knoweth me, that I am the Lord which exercise lovingkindness, judgment, and righteousness, in the earth: for in these things I delight, saith the Lord.

Jeremiah 9:23,24

In order to become pregnant, you first have to be able to conceive. The reason some can't conceive is that they're convinced that God can never use them. After all, they don't have much education. Surely, nobody would listen to them. They're just not the type. So they remain barren.

But I beg to differ. I dropped out of school in the eleventh grade, and Lawrence and I got married. Fifteen months later, I had a baby girl, and about two years after that I had another baby, a boy this time. Six years after that, I had another girl, and four years after that I had a third baby girl.

But all of that time, I was pregnant with something else. At the age of fourteen, when I got saved, I experienced God implanting a seed in my womb—the desire to preach. It didn't start to come to fulfillment until I was thirty-eight years old. Still, at that point, I hadn't had any further education—not a single day of seminary—and all I'd done was be a mama to my four children. Still, at that age, I stood and preached my first sermon.

It is only in knowing God that we are qualified to be impregnated with His desire and then to carry it to term. Those who pray without desire are praying vain, repetitious, and empty prayers, and I'm afraid that God doesn't even hear them. They've lost their *"first love,"* and they need to return to God's altar and get new fire in their souls.

If you're serious with God, get on your face before Him in prayer. Cry out for that gift to be manifested in your life. Wail and lament. Pray and take back what the devil has stolen from you. Bear down and push your way through to victory. Refuse to allow hell to have what is yours. It's time to bring forth life, and your work won't be finished until you have delivered it.

Commit to pray for those things that have weighed heavily on your heart. Pray as if life itself depended on your fervency. Pray like there is no tomorrow, for everything depends on how you pray—on your commitment to pray. It's time to live and pray like we believe God's Word regarding prayer.

We do not know truly that our Lord is the ground from which our prayer springeth–nor do we know that it is given us by his grace and his love. If we knew this, it would make us trust to have of our Lord's gifts all that we desire.

Juliana of Norwich

TWENTY-EIGHT

Desire Demands Desperation

Let the priests, the ministers of the Lord, weep between the porch and the altar, and let them say, Spare thy people, O Lord, and give not thine heritage to reproach, that the heathen should rule over them.

Joel 2:17

Get ready to give birth to your desire. You've been through enough pain. Now it's time to bring your dream to reality.

If your son is away at war, let the spirit of travail take hold of you for him. Let the labor pains intensify. Give way to the lamentation and howling that is rising up from your soul today. I guarantee you that things will not be the same again in your life or his.

Cry out for that child. Wail and lament. Pray a hole right through hell and take back what the devil has stolen from you. Cry out! Let the hot tears flow! If you don't know what to say, then just groan!

Why are our children not saved? We haven't had enough desire for them to be saved. We have insisted on three square meals a day, and that has made our bodies very round, but we need to fast more. Desire demands it. Do whatever you have to do. Refuse to give up. Lift up your voice like a trumpet. This is not a prayer about "the sweet by and by." You have to **storm the gates of hell and take back what has been stolen.**

> *And from the days of John the Baptist until now the kingdom of heaven suffereth violence, and the violent take it by force.*
>
> Matthew 11:12

Get serious. You wouldn't allow another person to beat up on your baby, and yet you've stood by and watched as the devil stomped your children into the ground. It's time to say, "No more!" Take back what is rightfully yours.

Don't give up until you feel the labor pains subside. You're on the right track. The psalmist declared: "Weeping may endure for a night, but joy cometh in the morning." *(Psalm 30:5) Don't stop praying until you feel that spirit of joy coming upon you. It may come as waves of laughter. It may come as a blanket of peace. Then you'll know that the baby has come forth in the name of Jesus.*

Prayers are deathless. The lips that uttered them may be closed to death, the heart that felt them may have ceased to beat, but the prayers live before God, and God's heart is set on them and prayers outlive the lives of those who uttered them; they outlive a generation, outlive an age, outlive a world.

Edward McKendree (E.M.) Bounds

TWENTY-NINE

Your Desires Are Not Your Own

Grant thee according to thine own heart, and fulfill all thy counsel.

Psalm 20:4

What are you birthing? You are giving birth to your God-inspired desire.

Some of you may need to give birth to your healing. You've been sick much too long. When that baby comes forth, you'll find not only that you're personally healed, but also that you can now lay hands on other sick people and see them healed.

You're not just carrying a desire for personal healing; your spiritual pregnancy will bring forth a gift of healing. Some of you will become prophets and prophetesses through travail. For a long time now, you've been carrying a desire to prophesy. That desire is from God. Bring it forth.

Some of you carry a desire to teach or a desire to preach. Those thoughts are not your own. They're God's desires implanted within your spirit. Now God wants to bring that gift forth, so don't give up until you feel it happen.

Lift your voice as loud as you can, and begin to pray in the Holy Ghost. When you do that, your prayers go straight to the throne of God. This makes sure the devil is powerless to block them.

He has told you that you'll never get what you are believing for, but he's a liar. God is about to do something in you that He's never done before. **When we wait upon God, answers come. Your destiny comes to life.**

Once the travail has ended and the desire has come forth, it's time to celebrate. It's time to give God the praise due to His name. Get excited, and let the world know that you've been delivered. You have something to shout about, so take your liberty. God has been good to you, so let Him know that you appreciate it.

He is a celebrating God, and you can be sure that all of heaven is celebrating with you. You have given birth to your desire, and there is an inseparable link between your desire and your destiny.

What is God attempting to birth in you? Sometimes the most profound thing we can do is to reflect on God's handiwork in our lives. Be mindful of how He is ordering your steps, the opportunities He has made possible, the connections He has orchestrated, the grace and capabilities He has bestowed—don't take for granted all that is transpiring in your life—but give thanks. Be grateful for all He is bringing to pass.

Faith sees the invisible, believes the unbelievable, and receives the impossible.

Corrie Ten Boom

THIRTY

The Source of Spiritual Desire

As for me, God forbid that I should sin against the Lord in ceasing to pray for you.

1 Samuel 12:23

I firmly believe that prayerlessness is one of the greatest sins of the American church today. It's a sin against man, just as much as it's a sin against God, and we're all guilty of this sin to some degree. We've all fallen short in this area.

But some have fallen so far short in regard to prayer that their spiritual lives are endangered. Or is it just the opposite? Has their spiritual lukewarmness caused them to become lazy about prayer? Whatever the case, prayerlessness has caused many to turn back from serving God and to serve their own flesh. It's time that we recognize the seriousness of this sin and do something about it.

What exactly is prayer? *Strong's Concordance* says it is "to entreat or go to." Prayer, then, is the way we get to God, the way we communicate with Him, the way we hear from Him and He hears from us. It also includes our praise and worship directed to Him.

Because of this, prayer is to the spirit what breath is to the body. If you stop breathing, you can't live long—probably only a matter of seconds. And it's the same way with prayer. Stop praying long enough, and you'll die spiritually. That's all there is to it.

If we are cut off from the very source of life, what can we expect? This is the reason that prayerlessness is such a grievous sin, one that God hates. Everything about our life hinges on prayer. John Wesley once said, "I pray two hours every morning. That is if I don't have a lot to do. If I have a lot to do for that day, then I pray three hours."

Abraham Lincoln said, "If I had eight hours to chop down a tree, I'd spend six of those hours sharpening my axe."

That's what we all need to do, spend some time sharpening our sword. Then it will be much easier to get things accomplished in life. Determine today that you will avoid the deadly sin of prayerlessness.

Look at your prayer life. What do you see? Ask the Lord to guide you into a deeper fellowship with Him. Whatever your prayer habits, there is a deeper place to go in your communion with the Living God. Ask the Lord to take you there—submit yourself to God that He might lift you up into the Holy of Holies today—seek to know Him more fully, to feel the penetrating magnitude of His greatness, and His grace.

The true man of God is heartsick, grieved at the worldliness of the Church. . . grieved at the toleration of sin in the Church, grieved at the prayerlessness in the Church. He is disturbed that the corporate prayer of the Church no longer pulls down the strongholds of the devil.

Leonard Ravenhill

THIRTY-ONE

The Dissipation of Desire

To him that knoweth to do good, and doeth it not, to him it is sin.

James 4:17

Usually, when we think of sin, we think of overt acts of disobedience to God. Surely prayer could not be placed in that same category. Or could it?

First, prayerlessness is what we call a sin of omission. We can sin by doing something wrong, but we can also sin by not doing something we should be doing.

Sins of omission don't seem very serious to us, but because this particular sin of omission weakens your spiritual life, making you less useful to God and more vulnerable to spiritual loss, nothing could be more serious.

If nothing else moves you in this regard, consider the personal loss that can come to you through prayerlessness. Look at it from a selfish viewpoint, if you will. **Prayerlessness will clearly rob you of many of the good things God has in store for you.** Is that serious enough for you? May the Lord bring each of us to repentance and renewal in this matter so that we can not only live the abundant life He has ordained for us here, but also further His kingdom on the earth.

Prayerlessness, however, is not just a sin of omission. God has called us to pray for many things specifically, and when we fail to do that, we're neglecting our responsibility and directly disobeying our heavenly Father. This grieves His heart and puts at risk our future relationship with Him.

Webster's Dictionary defines *neglect* as "to omit by carelessness or by design; to ignore or disregard; to fail to care for or attend to." When you fail to obey God in His commands concerning your prayer life, you signal to Him not only that you are careless about the matters of your soul, but also that you have decided to ignore and disregard His commands. You're not willing to attend to His business in your life.

Prayerlessness also makes you unavailable to God. He can't use people who fail to communicate with Him on a regular basis. How can you know the will of God for your life today if you haven't asked Him? How can you even know Him without the benefit of regular intimate communication with Him?

Holy Spirit, make me hungry for more of You! Cause me to thirst for Your Spirit! I invite You to awaken my heart to Your Presence in this moment now. Knit my heart to Yours—teach me to worship You in spirit and truth—and to seek You more passionately. Mold me and make me a vessel for Your honor prepared for every good work.

Prayer is an ordinance of God, that must continue with a soul so long as it is on this side glory.

John Bunyan

THIRTY-TWO

Romance and Desire

And then will I profess unto them, I never knew you: depart from me, ye that work iniquity.

Matthew 7:23

It's one thing to know someone from a distance, but it's quite another thing to know them intimately. I may feel that I know a certain popular preacher because I've seen them on television or been in one of their meetings, but do they know who I am or have we carried on a personal conversation? That's a different question entirely.

God knows those who know Him. This is the reason He declares to some, *"I never knew you."*

Prayerlessness is a serious sin because it says to God that you now have very little love left for Him. You may well protest that point, but the truth is that if you loved Him more, you would also love to talk to Him. **When you love**

someone, you enjoy communicating with them, and you take whatever time is necessary for it.

It's communication on every level that brings people together. If you and I were friends, and I hadn't seen you for a long time, I might have to say, "We used to be good friends. In fact, there was a time that we talked every day. But we're not very close anymore." The difference would be obvious.

Are there "good friends" who don't speak to each other for years at a time? I don't think so. In the same way, maybe you *used* to know God. But if you're not communicating with Him on a regular basis now, can you still say that you know Him?

Maybe you knew God's heart at one time, but is that still true? If you just show up once a week at His house and wave at Him from afar, that doesn't sound like love to me. It's never difficult or cumbersome to talk with someone you love.

Don't let prayerlessness rob you of the abundant life Jesus died for you to have. Determine to make it a priority and incorporate it into your daily routine at all cost. Rise a little earlier, turn the TV off a little sooner, walk and talk with the Lord whenever possible. Let Him know how much you love and appreciate Him.

Prayer as a relationship is probably your best indication about the health of your love relationship with God. If your prayer life has been slack, your love relationship has grown cold.

John Piper

THIRTY-THREE

Desires New Every Morning

It is of the Lord's mercies that we are not consumed, because his compassions fail not. They are new every morning.

Lamentations 3:22,23

Samuel Chadwick once said: "The crying need of the church is her laziness after God. The church needs nothing other than prayer because everything else follows prayer."

Andrew Murray, the great man of prayer himself, said, "The sin of prayerlessness is proof that the life of God and the soul is in deadly sickness and weakness."

E. M. Bounds, a man of prayer and a teacher on prayer, has said, "Prayer, much prayer, is the price of the anointing. Prayer, much prayer, is the sole condition of keeping it. Without this unceasing prayer, the anointing never comes. Without perseverance in prayer, the anointing, like manna overkept, breeds worms."

God has said that His mercies are *"new [fresh] every morning."*

It isn't how much I prayed last night. It's how much I've prayed since I got up this morning. We need to wake up thanking God for His mercies, thanking Him that we were able to sleep, that we had no pain in our bodies, and that we still have a sound mind. He kept us all night when hell could have destroyed us.

We need to wake up thanking God for being our Guide for the day, for walking with us and protecting us. We should thank Him all day long. Only praying lips are anointed lips.

Prayerlessness grieves the heart of God because a prayerless person is a carnal person. You can talk to some people for a few minutes and sense whether or not they've been in recent contact with God. If what comes out of their mouth is only foolishness, that's a good indication of prayerlessness.

Praying people always have exciting things to talk about. They can't wait to tell you what their prayers have wrought. They're expectant people because they have many petitions outstanding, and they can hardly wait to see what God will do next.

The Holy Spirit is the spirit of prayer, and one of His functions is to pray for us and with us. But when we become prayerless, He is grieved and often retreats. Some Christians suddenly wake up one day to find that the Holy Spirit is no longer with them. They used to speak in tongues now and again, but they haven't used this gift in a while now. Have you stirred up this precious gift lately? Have you called to Him and wooed Him to your private chamber to spend time alone with you today?

A man in love, or a woman in love will never quit. I want my life to be characterized by an unrestrained affection for the Son of God.

Jack Deere

THIRTY-FOUR

Desire Prays Through

And it came to pass in those days, that he went out into a mountain to pray, and continued all night in prayer to God.

Luke 6:12

In previous generations, it was not uncommon at all for children to overhear their parents crying out to God. When Lawrence and I first got married, we had a neighbor who lived across the street from us, and we heard her praying every single night. My own mother-in-law was a person who cried out to God aloud, and we often overheard her praying for hours at a time, and my mother was always a strong woman of prayer as well.

Most modern American Christians know nothing of "praying through." We get up in the morning, quickly ask the Lord to bless us and ours, and then we're off to our activities of the day. **"Praying through" means that you get**

God's heart, and then you stay in His presence, travailing in prayer, until the answer comes.

When we're determined to "pray through," we're never rushed to "get through" with our prayers. We're willing to stay right there, and we want to stay right there, until the victory comes. Today, when people pray at all, they keep looking at their watch. "Is my fifteen minutes up yet?" they want to know. "Oh, no. I've only prayed for thirteen minutes. I still have two more minutes to go." But that's not praying through.

When you pray through, you won't want to stop praying. You'll begin to see things as God sees them. You may even cry out like Isaiah, and say, "Lord, if You need someone to send, send me. I know that I'm not worthy, but I'm willing."

If we fail to pray, how can we discover the heartbeat of Jesus? It's worth discovering. When you've discovered it, you'll find that it's much bigger than your own. Prayerfulness makes you a bigger person, but prayerlessness makes you selfish.

When we have God's heart, we rejoice when others are healed, just as if we had been healed ourselves. We have just begun to know God's heart, and we all have a lot to learn in this regard. What are we waiting for? Cast off prayerlessness, and get your soul on fire for God once again.

When was the last time you "prayed through?" What is something in your life that might require you to pray a hole through to heaven? What is God's heart for a particular situation in your life that He might be waiting on you to grasp hold of more fervently? This might be the time to awake from your sleep...redeem the time, understand what the will of the Lord is, and be filled with the Spirit... praying always with all prayer. (Ephesians 5:14-18; 6:18)

If I have no love for others, no desire to serve others and I'm only concerned about my needs, I should question whether Christ is really in my life.

Rick Warren

THIRTY-FIVE

Prayer: The Breath of Desire

Pray one for another.

James 5:16

It's a scary thing when a person experiences a shortness of breath. They feel like they're dying—even if they're not. And all too often, they actually are dying. For instance, those who experience a blockage of the arteries and require bypass surgery (or, better yet, healing from God), first experience shortness of breath. Before long, it's a struggle for them just to walk a few steps. This is a very serious condition, and if they don't get help, they may die.

That's how serious this condition of prayerlessness is for any individual and for the church as a whole. As we have seen, when prayerlessness invades our world, we're being cut off from the source of all life. So it's no wonder that prayerless people often stop going to church. It's a struggle for them just to stay alive. No wonder they stop going to prayer meetings! They're struggling for life itself.

When you can't breathe, everything becomes more difficult.

Not only can't you run; you can hardly walk. Some can't even crawl. And the saddest thing of all is that they sit idly by as what little life they still have ebbs out of them. It's time to cry out to God before it's too late.

One of the most serious ways in which prayerlessness robs us is in the area of God's guidance for our lives. If we no longer have His guidance, we may be stumbling around in the dark, going nowhere fast and not even know it.

Prayerlessness also robs us of God's power in our lives. We need His hand reaching out to meet our every need, and when that hand is absent, we're in serious trouble.

To me, one of the worst things about prayerless Christians is that they are so selfish. And that's understandable. When we don't feel God's heart, we cannot help but become selfish in our prayers.

The Christian life is to be lived for others, and Christ set the example for us. **Learning to pray unselfishly will release fresh water into your life** and bring you many other benefits.

Make a commitment to actively pray every day for the next week. Make it a priority. The more you pray, the more you'll want to. The longer you pray, the longer you'll want to! Look forward to your prayer time with great anticipation—knowing God will meet you there. It will become the best part of your day and you won't be able to do anything else until you have prayed. Taste and see, the Lord is good!

The natural life knows that if the spiritual life gets hold of it, all its self-centeredness and self-will are going to be killed and it is ready to fight tooth and nail to avoid that.

C.S. Lewis

THIRTY-SIX

A Spare-Tire Desire

Praying always with all prayer and supplication in the Spirit, and watching thereunto with all perseverance and supplication for all saints.

Ephesians 6:18

Start developing your prayer life now. Real prayer cannot begin the day you're told that you have cancer or you have to undergo open-heart surgery, and it can't begin the day you're served with divorce papers. It takes time to develop a relationship with God, just as it does with any other person. And you can't just use Him like you do a spare tire.

Spare tires are important, and we all want to know that we have one. Any time we experience a flat with one of our four main tires, we get out the spare and put it on, and it serves us well until the other tire is repaired. When we have a flat tire, we're awfully glad to find that we have a viable spare. But soon enough, we put the spare tire back in the trunk and forget about it until the next crisis comes along. When things are going well, we don't need it.

Is God just a spare tire to you? Do you use Him only when you have an emergency? Speaking for myself, God has done so much for me already that if He never did another thing for me, still my lips would have to continually praise Him. I can't wait for some emergency to come along to begin building my prayer life. I have to do it now.

Building up your prayer life is a lot like doing weight training. You may not see the results immediately. Doing one session of weight training and then staring into the mirror to see the benefit would be foolish. It takes a while. Within six weeks, the change can be obvious and dramatic. And the longer you do weight training the easier it becomes. Something that seems heavy for you at the beginning will eventually feel very light, and you'll be able to lift more and more.

When we first begin to pray, we may receive only power to heal headaches, but when we persevere in prayer, the power to heal cancer will come. **Once you've developed a life of prayer, demons**

will have to obey you in the name of Jesus. Your very presence will send them scurrying.

God fully intended for prayer to be the great power by which His church operates. We can organize and reorganize, but nothing much will happen. We can do things that bring in big crowds, but nothing much will happen. It takes intense prayer to bring revival. In the words of Corrie Ten Boom, "Is prayer your steering wheel or your spare tire?"

Oh! men and brethren, what would this heart feel if I could but believe that there were some among you who would go home and pray for a revival – men whose faith is large enough, and their love fiery enough to lead them from this moment to exercise unceasing intercessions that God would appear among us and do wondrous things here, as in the times of former generations.

Charles Haddon Spurgeon

THIRTY-SEVEN

The Lifeline of Desire

And a certain man drew a bow at a venture, and smote the king of Israel between the joints of the harness: wherefore he said unto the driver of his chariot, Turn thine hand, and carry me out of the host; for I am wounded.

1 Kings 22:34

You have to give the king of Syria credit. He had a great battle plan when he went out to war against the kings of Israel and Judah. He instructed his men to ignore, for the most part, the opposing generals, lieutenants, and captains and go after King Ahab himself. They should attempt to kill him early in the battle. This would quickly demoralize the enemy and insure victory over them.

Ahab also recognized what a great strategy this was, and when he was wounded early in the battle by a well-placed arrow, he asked not to be taken away from the scene of the battle. Instead, his driver pulled to the side and propped the king up in his chariot. All day long, as the battle raged, the king's lifeblood drained out of him onto the floor of his chariot, but he stubbornly refused to retreat from the scene. If the enemy (or even his own men) knew that he was dying, the battle would be over.

That evening, the king died anyway, and the battle was over.

What a great strategy: kill the king, and the armies will be demoralized and scatter in confusion! When I read this passage again a few years ago, it suddenly dawned on me that this is Satan's strategy against the church today. If he can rob us of our Source of life, he can gradually weaken us until we no longer pose any threat to him or his kingdom. What is that one thing upon which our victory depends? It can only be our prayer life, our connection to the Source of everything we need. And if Satan can cut that connection, he can easily defeat us.

Prayer is our umbilical cord, attaching us to the life of God. **Prayer is our life-support system, pumping His life into us when we have none of our own.** If we can stay hooked up to the system, we can live. But if that connection is disturbed for any length of time, that will soon be the end of us.

Father God, help me to stay connected! Show me where the enemy has cut my lifeline and help me reconnect to You—the Source of life I so desperately need. Holy Spirit, help me not to grieve You, but to be led by You in all things, at all times.

The devil is not terribly frightened of our human efforts and credentials. But he knows his kingdom will be damaged when we begin to lift up our hearts to God.

Jim Cymbala

THIRTY-EIGHT

The Demise of Desire

And the battle increased that day: and the king was stayed up in his chariot against the Syrians, and died at even: and the blood ran out of the wound into the midst of the chariot.

1 Kings 22:35

What King Ahab did when he was wounded was not a wise thing. In fact, it was just a delaying tactic, and it worked only for a few hours. Because he had himself propped up, he looked to most people as if he was still alert and ready to aid in the battle. But the truth was that his life force was slowly being drained from him, and he wouldn't last long.

In the same way, it may seem wise to some in the church today to pretend that everything is all right when it's not, but the pretense can't last long. Soon enough, the truth will be known. **If your life has become prayerless, you may successfully hide that fact for a while, but eventually the truth will come out.**

As his strength ebbed away, remaining upright in his chariot must have become more and more of a strain for King Ahab. The amazing thing is that he was able to carry out the sham for an entire day. By evening, he could hold out no longer. His strength was gone. He died, and everyone soon knew the truth about him.

When prayer has become nothing more than a habit, we're in trouble. When prayer has been boiled down to a three-minute recitation to God before we go to sleep each night, we're in trouble. When prayer becomes simply a means of salving our conscience, we're in trouble.

Prayerlessness affects the individual, and then it begins to affect the whole church. Programs without prayer are just programs. There's no power in them. When prayer dies, it's not long before the gifts of the Spirit stop manifesting in our midst, the supernatural disappears, and there's no more prophecy and discernment. When prayer dies, preaching suffers. The truth is suddenly replaced with comforting platitudes.

Just as happened with King Ahab, Satan struck a master blow to America when, through the court system, he successfully barred prayer from our classrooms. Today, those same classrooms are full of hell and not nearly enough education. Our children are now involved in drugs, alcohol, sex, and even murder. What can we expect? The end of those who forget God will never be a pretty one.

Lord, forgive me for not seeking You as I should. Forgive me for standing idly by as the enemy shot at prayer and made inroads into the life of our nation. I am but one person, but use me to stand in the gap and intercede on behalf of this country. Amen.

Our prayers may be very beautiful in appearance and might appear to be the very paragon of devotion, but unless there is a secret spiritual force in them, they are vain things.

Charles Haddon Spurgeon

THIRTY-NINE

Desire Demands You Draw Aside

I wait for the Lord, my soul does wait, and in His word do I hope.

Psalm 130:5

When Ahab realized that he was wounded, he should have withdrawn himself and/or his army immediately and sought help. It was only because he was a stubborn and arrogant man that he could not bring himself to do it. He simply had to act like everything was all right and go on with the planned battle.

That was a very foolish thing to do. When you're wounded, that's not the time to act like nothing has happened. Get help right away. This is a matter of life and death. Draw aside and get the assistance you need before it's too late.

This is not the time to be going to a movie with a friend. You flip through a hundred and eighty channels on your television, but nothing seems to satisfy. You go to the refrigerator, but can't find anything you want to eat. All the while your spirit is crying out for help, saying, "Take me to my God! I'm hungry. I'm thirsty. I need a fresh touch from heaven. Take me to my God." Hurry to God before your life drains out of you, and it's too late.

The busyness of our modern lifestyle plays into Satan's hands because it's not conducive to prayer. We live in a shake-and-bake, heat-and-eat, brown-and-serve, hurry-up-and-wait society, and we rush about all day from one activity to another. Then we get up the next day and start the same race all over again. In this context, even a three-minute prayer seems to be a sacrifice, but it's not enough.

Nothing can ever replace prayer. Nothing! Going to church is not enough. Paying your tithes is not enough. Satan doesn't care if you do those things. He just doesn't want you to have intimate contact with the God of the universe. He knows that prayerlessness on your part can give him the victory quicker than anything else, and he loves to sit back and watch you bleed. He loves it when the king is dying, then he can have his way.

Run to God and put prayer back in its rightful place in your life: as king.

Pray the Lord draws you to Himself today. Pray that no enemy, no distraction, no legitimate excuse of any kind would keep you from dynamic contact with the Living God. Don't get so busy working for the Lord that you forget the Lord of the work. Be still, and know that He is God!

There is no effort comparable to prayer to God. In fact, whenever you want to pray, hostile demons try to interrupt you. Of course they know that nothing but prayer to God entangles them. Certainly when you undertake any other good work, and persevere in it, you obtain rest. But prayer is a battle all the way to the last breath.

Agathon

FORTY

Desiring the Joy of God's Presence

Thou wilt shew me the path of life: in thy presence is fulness of joy; at thy right hand there are pleasures for evermore.

Psalm 16:11

All of us, ministers and lay people alike, need time in God's presence. In His presence, there is *"fulness of joy."*

Joy has also been equated to *"strength"*:

The joy of the Lord is your strength.

Nehemiah 8:10

When you linger in God's presence, wounds are healed, and all that you need for life is poured into you. Your flabby muscles are strengthened, and suddenly you become a threat to Satan and his kingdom. He will do absolutely anything to prevent that from happening. He doesn't want you hooked up to that lifeline. He wants to see you drained of life so that you're no longer a threat to him.

God created us for constant communication with Him. After He had created Adam and Eve, He came down in the cool of the day and walked and talked with them. Can you imagine God coming to your house one morning, knocking on your door, and saying, "Come on, let's have a walk so that we can talk some things over"? Wouldn't that be wonderful? Would you ever dare to say to Him, "I'm too busy. Let me get the kids off to school first. Then, as soon as I finish the dishes and my conference call to the office, we can talk"?

God created us for fellowship, and yet modern man has become too busy to have the kind of fellowship with God that He envisioned when He created us. In this way, the very reason for our creation has been thwarted by our own willfulness and coldness of spirit.

"I'm too busy," may sound legitimate, but we're all creatures of habit, and we can develop good habits and bad habits. "I don't have time," is just an excuse. We have time for what we want to have time for. Admit it and ask God to help you reserve more time for Him.

Father, help me to make more time for You. Shake me awake in the morning and call out to me at night—and then give me ears to hear and a willing heart quick to respond! Close my ears to any other voice but Yours. I thank You, Lord, that where I am weak, You are strong—for I can do nothing unless You do it through me. Thank You for Your Spirit at work in me causing me to will and to do Your good pleasure.

Prayer does not mean asking God for all kinds of things we want, it is rather the desire for God Himself, the only Giver of Life.

Sadhu Sundar Sing

FORTY-ONE

Determine Your True Desire

Know ye not that the friendship of the world is enmity with God?

James 4:4

I wasted many years of my life trying to blame my failures on someone else or something else. "If only I hadn't married a man who was so dedicated to business," I thought many times. "If only I had gone on to get more education, perhaps then I could have done something more for God." What a waste of time this kind of thinking proved to be! When I got serious with God in prayer, He showed me where my problem was. It was in me.

I had two neighbors whose husbands sometimes traveled with Lawrence, and I would spend a lot of time with them. Although they were morally upright, they were not churchgoing people, and we had little in common.

I went to church on Sundays and Wednesdays and took my children with me, but otherwise my spiritual life seemed to be going nowhere. “Why aren’t You using me more, Lord?” I would ask Him almost every morning. I knew that I was called, but my calling seemed to be stalled.

When I finally saw what the problem was, I was shocked. I was like King Ahab, dying, and just propped up for the sake of appearance. I needed to make some major changes in my life.

One of the first things I had to do was to be more careful about the company I kept. Too much time with my friends and not enough time with God was holding me back. I had to make a hard decision about my friends.

There are some people in our lives whom we can hold on to for just so long. Then we have to let them go. If we are willing to break some unhealthy relationships, God will give us better ones. Thinking back to those former times, and considering the kind of people I now call my friends—the Juanita Bynams, the Paula Whites, the Rod Parsleys, the T. D. Jakes of this world—look where God has brought me from.

If I had insisted on holding on to my old friends, I would still be doing the same old things today. **There are some people and some things that we have to let go of if we are to make any progress in life.** And our choices in this regard reflect the depth of our spiritual desire.

Lord, show me those distractions that are holding me back and help me let them go in a peaceable way. I trust You, Lord, to do what's best and thank You now for the seasons I have had with certain friends or relatives, the blessing they have been to me for a time, and for all the rich friendships and purposeful endeavors that are yet in store.

The degree of blessing enjoyed by any man will correspond exactly with the completeness of God's victory over him.

A.W. Tozer

FORTY-TWO

Delighting Daily in Spiritual Desire

But his delight is in the law of the Lord; and in his law doth he meditate day and night.

Psalm 1:2

When we have developed a prayer life, we don't have to call a dozen people about every problem we encounter in life. We're hooked up to the heavenly lifeline, and nothing is hindering the flow of blessing between God and us.

This is the reason it's so important to repent quickly when we know that we have displeased God in any way. This keeps the window of blessing always open. Sin can too easily separate us from God.

Don't let anything keep you from prayer. We may go for a day or two without prayer, and no one will know, but when we go four or five days without it, our spouse and children will know. And when we've gone a week or two without it, everyone will know. You may sit propped up for a while, but as the life drains from you, eventually you will collapse, and everyone will become painfully aware of your failure.

There is a thrill to be experienced in the presence of God. Don't miss it. One night Lawrence and I were out visiting some friends, and it began to get late. By the time we got home, it was already eleven thirty. I told Lawrence, "You've made me miss my appointment with the Lord," but I was just kidding though. I knew that we would pray anyway, even though we were late getting started.

When we arrived at the house, my good friend Arlene, who lives with us, had the lights down low and the music playing. As I walked in, I felt a wonderful presence of the Lord that brought tears to my eyes. Nothing can compare to God's presence.

I look forward to my quiet times with the Lord. How wonderful, when it's just Him and me! When people tell me that they never hear from God, I know immediately that they have no proper prayer life. No Christian can afford to go any length of time without hearing His voice.

When we fall out of love with Jesus and prayer suddenly becomes drudgery, a constant struggle, a dread rather than a delight, Satan is delighted. He's not so worried when we memorize the Bible. He knows it too—a lot better than most of us do. His one goal is to cut us off from communication with the Author of the Word of Life. Don't let it happen.

Lord Jesus, my heart hungers for more of You in every moment of my life. Daily I run to You! Daily fill me with Your Spirit, surround me with Your Presence, overtake me with Your Love. I want to hear Your voice, feel Your touch, and know Your heart like never before.

Nothing means so much to our daily prayer life as to pray in the name of Jesus. If we fail to do this, our prayer life will either die from discouragement and despair or become simply a duty which we feel we must perform.

Ole Kristian O. Hallesby

FORTY-THREE

Owning Your Desire

And we know that all things work together for good to them that love God, to them who are the called according to his purpose.

Romans 8:28

I remember every detail of the day things turned around in my own life. I had been shopping that day and I bought a new dress. When I got home, Jana saw the dress and said to me, "Mom, you already have a dress just like that." I couldn't imagine that she was right, but to prove her point, she went into my closet and came out holding the dress in question.

Sure enough, I had bought a dress exactly like one I already had in the closet. I was shocked. So this was what my life had become, an endless shopping spree? Without delay or pretense, I went into my bathroom, fell on my face before the Lord, and began to confess that

I was the problem, not Lawrence, and not anyone else.

From that moment on, I determined, rather than trying to blame someone or something else for my failure, I would pursue the Lord as I knew I should have been pursuing Him all along. Whatever He wanted me to do, that's what I would do. But most of all, I would spend time alone with God.

From that day on, whenever I had an urge to go shopping, I would pick up my Bible and begin to study it, and I would take the time to pray. With this, the Bible soon became my daily bread, and my time with God became my strength.

And many other things began to change. Within six months after I made that commitment and began that new kind of prayer life, Lawrence had a Damascus Road experience one day and was totally changed. I was, and still am, convinced that God would have dealt with him much sooner if I had gotten my own act together sooner. When I acted, God acted. That must mean that He's waiting for us, and the failure is ours, never His.

Become obsessed with God, with His kingdom, with His will, and with His Word, and

when you do, you'll find that *"all things work together for good."*

Father God, I love You with all that I am. I need You more than the air I breathe. I can't imagine having to take a breath on this earth without the knowledge of You and Your love alive in my very own heart. You mean more to me than anything I could ever dream.

Prayer is not a matter of getting what we want the most. Prayer is a matter of giving ourselves to God and learning His laws, so that He can do through us what He wants the most.

Agnes Sanford

FORTY-FOUR

Hold Tight to Your Desire

And thou shalt love the Lord thy God with all thine heart, and with all thy soul, and with all thy might.

Deuteronomy 6:5

The day Lawrence and I began pursuing God with all that was within us, our lives began to turn around dramatically. We went to church every time the doors were open. We arrived early and stayed late. We performed willingly and cheerfully anything that was asked of us. And God began to take care of us in ways we had not experienced before.

If you love God and are interested in His kingdom and His will, He'll do the same for you. But if you continue to live in the same old way day after day, week after week, and month after month, seeing the same old friends, entertaining the same old habits, seeing the same movies and reading the same books, playing the same games and living the same lifestyle, then don't expect God to do something different for you. You've made your choice.

Many Christians are sure that miracles ceased with the apostles, but the truth is that miracles cease when we stop praying. There's no substitute for prayer, and if Satan can succeed in killing your prayer life, then it's over.

I sometimes think back and wonder what I might have done for the kingdom if I had given the Lord the fifteen years I wasted doing my own thing. If I had been in pursuit of God during those fifteen years like I have in the past twenty years, there's no telling what could have been accomplished. **Don't allow the things of life to crowd out your spirituality.** Our modern lives are often cluttered with seemingly legitimate things. They may not be sins in themselves, but the sin is that they rob us of the time we need to spend with God.

You do go to church, but other than that limited time which you have successfully allotted for the Lord, He has been crowded out of your life. Then you wonder why sickness or financial trouble comes, and you're compelled to cry out to God. This may be the only way the Lord can get your attention.

He has already provided for your healing, and He has already provided for your financial rescue because He knows that there will be times when He will have to force you to need His intervention. Otherwise, His will is that you remain well and financially blessed.

Look at your life today. Are you pursuing God with all your heart and all your strength? How could you intensify your pursuit of Him? What will you do today to move to higher ground with the Lord? What do you think will change as a result?

Prayer is not merely an occasional impulse to which we respond when we are in trouble: prayer is a life attitude.

Walter A. Mueller

FORTY-FIVE

Hunger, Thirst, and Desire

O God, thou art my God; early will I seek thee: my soul thirsteth for thee, my flesh longeth for thee in a dry and thirsty land.

Psalm 63:1

In recent years, I've traveled a lot in ministry, and Lawrence travels a lot with his business, and sometimes I get so hungry just to talk to him and hear him talk to me. He feels exactly the same way. Sometimes he says to me, "Can we just sit down for a few minutes. We haven't had time to talk in days. Can we just do nothing but talk for a while?"

We do it, and it's wonderful. How much more this should be true of us spending time with our Lord.

How long has it been since you talked to Him, really talked to Him, shared your heart with Him, and "loved on" Him? I'm not talking about asking God for things. In your most intimate times with Him, you won't be able to think of a single thing you need.

Come aside, saints of God, and put first things first. If you're guilty of neglecting prayer, Satan will drag you down very quickly. If you've been wounded, turn aside quickly and get help. Don't risk allowing your life to ebb out of you.

We Christians sometimes get busy in religious activity—knocking on doors, handing out tracts, singing, and preaching. These are all good, but somehow prayer seems to get sacrificed. Many of those who attend our churches these days watch the clock, and if the preacher goes over thirty minutes, they get up and leave. They have somewhere to go, someone to meet, or something to eat. How sad! God is last on their list of important things to do, and they rarely seem to get to Him.

We're living in the midst of a pleasure-hungry society, and people all around us are rushing here and there to find satisfaction. Listen to the cry of your heart and His. He has longings, just like we do. He seeks love, just like we do. He's waiting to meet with you today.

Lord Jesus, You are welcome here in this place right now. Please come and be with me for a while as I so long to feel Your Presence. I will be still and wait patiently. You have waited for so many times and for so long, I can sit quietly for a bit a wait upon You…

I want deliberately to encourage this mighty longing after God. The lack of it has brought us to our present low estate. The stiff and wooden quality about our religious lives is a result of our lack of holy desire.

C.S. Lewis

FORTY-SIX

Nothing Can Separate You from Your Desire

I was in the Spirit on the Lord's day, and heard behind me a great voice, as of a trumpet.

Revelation 1:10,11

When the apostle John was exiled to the Isle of Patmos, they stripped him of everything he possessed. They were sure that he had been immobilized, but they forgot one thing. They couldn't stop him from praying. He was praying one Lord's Day when a wonderful revelation came to him.

Although they had stripped John of everything, they were unable to cut off his direct link to heaven. Like John, I can say, "Take this whole world, but give me a life of prayer with the Lord. Let me ever cling to the horns of God's altar."

How long has it been since you stayed on your knees until you knew that victory had come? When the early disciples were imprisoned, they thanked God for the privilege to suffer for Him and then prayed that they would have boldness to continue. They had learned this life of prayer from Jesus himself. His custom was to rise early in the morning and go to a mountain where He could be alone with the Father. **If the very Son of God had to pull Himself aside to maintain life, how much more should we do the same?**

Oh, it will be a struggle to fight your flesh day in and day out, because it doesn't want to pray. Satan is behind that fight. He knows that you can conquer him in every other area but this one. He knows that the man or woman who prays is a man or woman of God who will fulfill his or her purpose in God. Search your heart today to see how you can effectively spend more time with God in prayer.

Let's get our list of important things in order. Let's make some necessary adjustments and find more time for God. Too many times, our heavenly Father calls, but no one answers. He speaks, but no one listens. His heart yearns, but no one responds. He's our God, and He has what we need, but He is waiting for us to come to Him as we should. Do it today.

Father, thank You for Your faithfulness toward me! Thank You Lord God for Your mercies new every morning, Your goodness and grace, Your righteousness and Truth! Early will I seek You and always will I long to find You! You alone are my one true heart's desire.

Prayer is talking with God and telling Him you love Him, conversing with God about all the things that are important in life, both large and small, and being assured that He is listening.

C. Neil Strait

FORTY-SEVEN

Above All, Desire Prayer

But if from thence thou shalt seek the Lord thy God, thou shalt find him, if thou seek him with all thy heart and with all thy soul.

Deuteronomy 4:29

Nothing has been done in the earth that hasn't come through prayer, **nothing supernatural has ever been accomplished without being preceded by prayer**, and there has never been a revival or a move of God that wasn't birthed through prayer. The Bible declares this truth in simplicity:

Ye have not, because ye ask not.

James 4:2

Prayer is our life force—it is the secret of tapping into the divine. So the question is, why are people not praying more in the twenty-first century?

I believe modern Americans are failing in the important responsibility of prayer because they simply don't know how to pray. Everything about our modern world is so technical and so well-defined and documented that they expect to have a detailed manual on correct prayer procedures. But the truth is that there is no one "correct" way to pray.

It's not wrong to read good books on prayer or listen to good sermons on prayer, but don't think that anyone can teach you the way you should pray personally. That's between you and God. You will develop it by doing it.

When people ask me how to pray, I tell them that they can learn just by doing it. Prayer is something that no one can really teach you to do and do well. Start praying, and be led by the Spirit.

Why is this true? It's because prayer is such a personal thing between you and God. It would be wrong for you to simply imitate the way others pray. You have to learn your own way of praying. No one had to teach me how to talk with my husband. Because we loved each other, we just did it. And we learned by doing.

One thing I know: the more you pray, the more you will want to pray, and the less you pray, the less you will want to pray. Get started, and you will improve.

Pray always and at all times. Pray without ceasing. With all supplications, and all prayers, let your requests be made known unto God. When you confess your sins, know that God hears you and is faithful to forgive. Praise Him continually and be continually filled with the Holy Spirit. Give thanks always for all things unto God the Father in the Name of Christ Jesus. Do everything as unto the Lord—and rejoice!

Oh, how strenuous is life! I know a little of it. Men "ought always to pray, and not to faint." How fierce the battle! I know something of the conflict, but I ought not to faint, because I can pray.

G. Campbell Morgan

FORTY-EIGHT

Desire What God Desires

And this is the confidence that we have in him, that, if we ask any thing according to his will, he heareth us: And if we know that he hear us, whatsoever we ask, we know that we have the petitions that we desired of him.

1 John 5:14,15

If your prayer life is being conducted selfishly, you're missing out on a great deal. It is still a greater blessing to give than it is to receive. Your prayer life should be centered around God's Kingdom, His will for you and others, His church and where it's going these days. Learn to pray His heart.

There is no biblical promise that, when we have prayed according to our own will, we can be confident of receiving an answer from God. Some people have been praying for years now for a better house, and they don't understand why God's not answering that prayer. That really bothers me. God wants you to have a good house, but that's not a subject worthy of your prayer focus. **Get your mind onto more important things, and your prayer life will become fruitful.**

Many times we don't even have to pray for material things. God just sends them our way. If we pray that His will be done on the earth and that His kingdom come, and we're doing all that we know to do to bring that about, He'll make things happen for us. His promise is clear:

> *Seek ye first the kingdom of God, and his righteousness; and all these things shall be added unto you.*
>
> Matthew 6:33

Learning to pray unselfishly will bring many new and wonderful benefits to your life.

According to 1 John 5:14, we can be confident that God hears what we say to Him in prayer only when we pray *"according to His will."* When we're off praying our own thing, asking for what we want and not what He wants, asking for things that we may even know are not good for us, thankfully, God doesn't even listen.

Lord God, make me a vessel of Your will. Cause me to think Your thoughts, dream Your dreams, and speak Your words. I want to be a person after Your own heart. Unite my heart to Yours and make me one with You. May there be less of me and more of You as I grow in You day by day. Thank You for Your Spirit of Truth living in me—that Your laws are written on my heart and Your Words are fitted to my mouth. How delicious is Your Word and how rich is Your Truth.

Let this be thy whole endeavor, this thy prayer, this thy desire–that thou mayest be stripped of all selfishness, and with entire simplicity follow Jesus only.

Thomas Kempis

FORTY-NINE

A Desire Unto Death

O my Father, if it be possible, let this cup pass from me.

Matthew 26:39

In the prayer of Jesus in Gethsemane, we have a perfect example of how we can pray in the will of God. Jesus was enjoying life and had every reason to live. He was not thrilled with the idea of giving His life on Calvary. Plus, what the Father was asking Him to do (take upon himself the sins of the whole world) was so terrible that He felt He simply could not bear it.

What was set before Jesus was so terrible to behold that His perspiration began to come as great drops of blood. Several times, He asked the Father if there might not be some other way to save mankind. Then suddenly something changed. As Jesus looked into the cup held out to Him by the Father, He saw something.

Personally, I've always believed that He saw people and their need for His sacrifice. He saw men and women locked in prisons with no hope for the future. He saw men and women with needles stuck in their veins, filling themselves with damaging drugs. He saw women selling their bodies in the streets of the cities of the world. When He saw all of that, His prayer changed, and He became willing to do whatever was necessary to save mankind. He prayed:

Nevertheless not as I will, but as thou wilt.

Matthew 26:39

Jesus was willing to drink that bitter cup so that those in prison could become preachers of the gospel, so that those shooting up drugs could become youth leaders, and so that those who once prostituted themselves on the streets could become Sunday school teachers. And so His mind was made up, and He was ready for the cross and ready for death. He was ready because He now understood the will of the Father, to bring redemption to all mankind. How could He oppose such a great purpose?

When your prayer changes from one that seeks only your own good to one that **seeks the good of God's kingdom** for the people around you, then **all of heaven will suddenly stand at attention**, and you will get results you have only dreamed of until now. If your prayers are not being answered, check to see if one of these might be the reason.

Oh Lord God, You are worthy of all praise, all worship, all sacrifice. I bow my knee to You. I fall on my knees and worship at Your throne. You alone are holy, You alone are worthy, You alone are mighty to be praised. You alone are my God.

I will die for my God. I will die for my faith. It's the least I can do for Christ dying for me.

Cassie Rene Bernall
(A 17-year-old from Columbine High School in Littleton, Colorado, who died April 20, 1999)

FIFTY

No Greater Desire

Bless the Lord, O my soul: and all that is within me, bless his holy name. Bless the Lord, O my soul, and forget not all his benefits.

Psalm 103:1,2

Another reason people don't pray today is because their priorities are all "messed up." This word *priority* means "precedence, especially established by order of importance or urgency."

A priority indicates the importance you place on something. Most Americans think first about their job and the income it provides for them. Next, they think about their family, about their house and car (and maybe the boat in the garage). Unfortunately, God is way down on their list of priorities, and so it's no wonder they don't have time to pray. Other things are more important to them.

Isn't it time that we made an appointment with God. These days, it seems that we have appointments for everyone and everything else in life except Him. Married couples even make an appointment (better known as a date) with each other in order to be able to spend meaningful time together.

If you'll make an appointment with God, I guarantee that He'll show up and be on time. Will you?

We have a common misconception because we talk about "waiting on God." That doesn't mean that He's not there. In reality, we're not waiting on Him; He's waiting on us.

Proper priorities demand that we take time to be alone with God. If those of us who are married don't spend time alone with our spouse, we won't make it as a couple. Time alone should be what we crave.

Let other things go for the moment. There will be time for them later. Take care of the more important things in life. God wants to talk to you. Give Him the time He deserves. How precious it should be to us that the God of the universe would say to us, "Come aside. I want to talk to you." Don't ever take that lightly.

Make time with God a priority, even if you have to write it on your calendar. If we just thought of God as a friend who we should regularly touch base with, it would be better than the little we meet with Him now. How much more if we truly understood Him to be the loving Father that He is, or the Lover of our souls that He longs to be.

The value of consistent prayer is not that He will hear us, but that we will hear Him.

William McGill

FIFTY-ONE

First Desire

Nevertheless I have somewhat against thee, because thou hast left thy first love. Remember therefore from whence thou art fallen, and repent, and do the first works; or else I will come unto thee quickly, and will remove thy candlestick out of his place, except thou repent.

Revelation 2:4,5

How did our priorities get so "messed up"? We're so attached to the things of this world. Yet these things will all fade away in time and, therefore, amount to very little. Of them, the Bible says, *"Which all are to perish with the using"* (Colossians 2:22). We're so intent on chasing the pleasures of this world, and yet we have not given God His rightful place. I'm afraid that it's because we've left our *"first love."*

In Revelation 2, Jesus spoke through John to the church at Ephesus. He commended them for the good things they were doing, but He went on to say that He had something against them. They had left their *"first love"* (Revelation 2:4). I used to preach that this only meant that they had stopped experiencing joy in attending church services, singing in the church choir, and hearing the preaching of the Word of God. But one day God showed me that it meant much more.

God showed it to me this way: Lawrence Bishop was my first love and the only man I ever said "I love you" to. Lawrence has richly blessed my life and has given me many wonderful things. No woman could ask for more. But what would happen if I, for some reason, started spending more time with the things Lawrence has given me and neglected to spend time with the person himself? That would be a tragic mistake, wouldn't it?

That's what happened at Ephesus. The people were doing a great work *for* God, but they were not doing enough *with* God. It's not enough that I travel all over the world *for* Him, preaching five to seven times a week and spending twenty to thirty hours a week studying the Scriptures in preparation for that ministry. I need to spend time *with*

God. **If I haven't spent quality time *with* God, then I'm neglecting my** *"first love."*

You can be going all the right places and doing all of the right things and still miss it. There must be a time when we come apart, go into some secret place, and say to the Lord, "There, Lord. Now it's just You and me."

Lord, here I am. I have nothing better to do than love on You. You are my heart's first desire. All I want to do is be with You right now. Let's just sit for awhile...I'm listening.

Knowledge about him will not do. Work for him will not do. We must have personal, vital fellowship with him; otherwise Christianity becomes a joyless burden.

John Piper

FIFTY-TWO

Desiring His Presence

Martha, Martha, thou art careful and troubled about many things: But one thing is needful: and Mary hath chosen that good part, which shall not be taken away from her.

Luke 10:41,42

When I'm on the road, there's always someone from our church accompanying me. Although I love their company, there come moments when I need some time alone with God, and I ask them to excuse themselves. The moment they close that hotel door, the presence of God floods the room, and although I may be a little hoarse from preaching, in those moments I sing to Jesus.

When was the last time you sang a song to the Lord? Oh, I know that you join in the congregational singing from time to time, but do you ever just sing to Him on your own, when no one else is listening? It doesn't matter if you can sing well or not. When you sing to Him, it sounds good to Him, and that's all that matters.

How long has it been? How long has it been since you said to the Lord, "I want to just sit here in Your presence and meditate on Your goodness. I just want to thank You, Lord, for everything You've done for me. You're such a good God. I thank You because of who and what You are to me."

When we say that a person has lost their *"first love,"* it doesn't mean that they no longer love anything about God. It's possible to love the trappings of Christianity and still not love the Christ of Christianity. It's possible to get so caught up in doing His work that we forget the Man behind the works.

We can give, we can love others, and we can hate sin, but if our heart isn't drawn to the presence of God, we simply don't love Him as we used to. There's no other way to explain it.

If you don't love being around a person it means that you don't love that person. What else can it mean? When you would rather be doing something else than staying in the presence of God, that's proof enough that you no longer love Him in the same way.

Nothing is more important than spending time with Him. Pursue time alone with Your God, seek His presence, sit at the foot of the throne for awhile. As hard as it is, put the demands of the day aside and practice being a Mary rather than a Martha. Choose the better part.

When the Spirit is absent, our excuses always seem right, but in the presence of the Spirit our excuses fade away.

R.T. Kendall

FIFTY-THREE

Childlike Desire

Verily I say unto you, Except ye be converted, and become as little children, ye shall not enter into the kingdom of heaven. Whosoever therefore shall humble himself as this little child, the same is greatest in the kingdom of heaven.

Matthew 18:3,4

We're God's children, and He's our Father, but if our lives reflect prayerlessness, that indicates to Him that we have become independent of Him and no longer need Him. Can this be right?

All children need their fathers. Children are dependant upon their fathers for every need and every decision. Children can't make decisions, and we're children. We desperately need our heavenly Father. Why don't we recognize that fact?

With the advance of modern psychology, we're discovering that the reason many people seem to have very warped personalities these days is that they lacked the meaningful participation of a father in their growing-up years. Such people have great difficulty understanding the place of God in their lives. They need to learn all over again what it means to have a father. And they must learn all over again how to be like a child in need of *the* Father.

In our churches these days, we often talk of the need to be born again, but once that is accomplished, we usually think that we're suddenly all grown up and can do things on our own. That's simply not the case. On another occasion, Jesus again showed His disciples the importance of being childlike:

> *And they brought young children to him, that he should touch them: and his disciples rebuked those that brought them. But when Jesus saw it, he was much displeased, and said unto them, Suffer the little children to come unto me, and forbid them not: for of such is the kingdom of God. Verily I say unto you, Whosoever shall not receive the kingdom of God as a little child, he shall not enter therein. And he took them up in his arms, put his hands upon them, and blessed them.*
>
> Mark 10:13-16

God's kingdom is made up of His children, and His children depend on Him for everything. What is required of us is to form a more loving and communicative bond with Him. We must acknowledge Him as our Father and give Him that special place in our lives.

Lord, help me to be more childlike. Help me to be more completely reliant on Your affection and approval. I look to You in all things for Your grace, guidance, provision, and mercy. I long to be Your favored child and to have memorable times together—to laugh and have fun and know that I am loved.

God does not stand afar off as I struggle to speak. He cares enough to listen with more than casual attention. He translates my scrubby words and hears what is truly inside. He hears my sighs and uncertain gropings as fine prose.

Timothy Jones

FIFTY-FOUR

Desire to Know the Voice of God

If any man hear my voice, and open the door, I will come in to him, and will sup with him, and he with me.

Revelations 3:20

We are in the process of being formed into the bride of Christ, and He will one day be joined to us in marriage, so that we can spend eternity with Him. But how can we hope to achieve that coveted position if we don't take time now to get to know Him better, to become intimate with Him? And how can we expect to escape the difficult times that will come upon the earth if we have neglected to build our relationship with God through prayer now? The times that are ahead will be as none other:

This know also, that in the last days perilous times shall come.

2 Timothy 3:1

If we are forced to face such times without knowing well the voice of God, we will surely find ourselves in serious trouble. **Listen to Him more now, so that you can recognize His voice later.**

How is it that we know the voice of our spouse, the voice of our children, and the voice of our friends, and yet we don't know the voice of God? We know the voice of popular singers, media personalities, and politicians, and yet we don't know the voice of God.

We know the popular voices of our day because that's what we listen to on a regular basis. We don't know God's voice because we don't listen to Him nearly enough.

This is serious. We are constantly under attack from hell, and we're being tempted and tried every day. Yet we go for weeks without ever calling on the name of the Lord, who is our strength. If we know that *"prayer . . . availeth much,"* why is it that we don't pray more? When we know God's promises that *"all things whatsoever we ask in prayer believing, we shall receive"* and that *"we have this confidence that if we ask anything that it shall be done,"* why don't we pray more?

Why don't we pray? Because we have not known how, because we have not been getting answer to prayers already prayed, and because our priorities have been all "messed up." But the worst indictment against us is that we don't pray because we've left our "first love."

Lord, help me to hear Your voice today. Help me to know Your voice as well as I know the voice of my loved ones. Give me ears to hear and a heart hungry for more of Your Presence. Teach me to walk in Your Truth so that I would not grieve You. Guide me into sweet fellowship with You that I might learn to heed only Your voice and no other.

Faith never knows where it is being led, but it loves and knows the One who is leading.

Oswald Chambers

FIFTY-FIVE

Don't Put Off Desire

Mine house shall be called an house of prayer for all people.

Isaiah 56:7

When we're young, we always think that we'll have plenty of time for God in the future. At the moment, we're full of vim and vigor, and there are so many things we need to experience in life. Later we plan to give God the time we know He deserves. But, for some odd reason, that time for developing a prayer life never seems to come. The reason is that as we age, nothing changes.

When you reach fifty, you feel as young as ever, and you still don't want life to pass you by. So you postpone your date with God for another decade or so. And another. And another.

This same pattern often continues, until one day people lie dying in some hospital bed. Only then do they wake up and realize that they have allowed life's most important things to pass them by, without laying hold of them. They are saddened. But, of course, it's too late. Please don't be one of those people.

He very much wants to manifest His glory in your life and to give you miracles on a daily basis. But that can't happen until you recognize Him as your source and seek Him in all things, until He can see that you're really in love with Him and want His presence with you. Are we ready to make God's house a house of prayer again, as He intended?

Are we ready to be the praying person God has called us to be? If so, we must humble ourselves before Him today. Bow in His presence, hungry for more of Him. Let Him know how very much you need Him, and ask Him to forgive you for having been too busy doing things that won't matter much in the light of eternity. Then take time to praise Him.

Where do you stand? Are your priorities right? Don't put off another day running to the throne of God and setting your heart right with you're Heavenly Father. Call out to Him now: "Father God, You are my number one priority. Let there only be You at the center of my heart's care. You are worthy of my undivided attention. Early I will seek You, all the day long will I praise You, and the beauty of Your holiness will be my last thought at night."

He will be unto thee a mighty pillar, bearing up heaven and earth, whereto thou mayst lean and not be deceived, wherein thou mayst trust and not be disappointed.

Robert Cawdray

FIFTY-SIX

Desire to Lay Aside Every Weight

Let us lay aside every weight, and the sin which doth so easily beset us, and let us run with patience the race that is set before us.

Hebrews 12:1

According to Strong's, this word *weight* means "a hindrance or burden." It's not necessarily something evil in itself, but it does evil by dulling your conscience and choking out the spirit of prayer in your life. A weight is anything that pulls you down and makes living for God more difficult for you. **When the Spirit of God begins to reveal to you the weights in your life, He'll also give you the power to lay them aside.** Then it's up to you. Anything that hinders the will of God in your life should be forsaken if you want to make spiritual progress. And that's true whether you consider a thing to be sin or not. Any weight, if it is not quickly cast off, will hold you down.

This passage of Scripture was clearly written to Christians, not sinners. To many sinners, the concept of sin has very little meaning. Those who are not believers in Christ, rarely if ever, consider their actions to be sin. For them, what they're doing is normal behavior. They're just doing what comes naturally, what's in their nature to do.

Sin is a Christian concept and can be understood only by those who long to do God's will and live a life pleasing to Him. A sinner may be able to stop some offensive behavior, but he can never stop being a sinner. That's what he is. Turning over a new leaf will not save him. By nature, he's a sinner, and unless God changes him, he'll always remain a sinner.

The concept of sin is very meaningful to those who know God. Only a believer in Christ can successfully lay aside weights and expect his or her life to change dramatically. So start laying aside the weights you discover, and don't stop until every weight has been dealt with.

Sin has a way of wrapping itself around you, and if its hold is not quickly broken, it will pull you down and smother you in the process. Sin will always take you further than you wanted to go and keep you longer then you wanted to stay. Most of us have one particular area of vulnerability, one area of special weakness, and this is what the Scriptures mean by *"the sin which doth so easily beset us."* You may not be tempted by the things that tempt others, but something draws you aside. If you follow it, it will lead you into other sins as well.

Lord, please show me where I have been complacent concerning Your Will, or slow to heed Your voice. Help me to replace any weights that have pulled me away from You with that which will draw me closer.

Indeed the safest road to Hell is the gradual one—the gentle slope, soft underfoot, without sudden turnings, without milestones, without signposts.

C.S. Lewis

FIFTY-SEVEN

The Weight of Distraction

So run, that ye may obtain.

1 Corinthians 9:24

For most of us, the struggle we're currently involved in is nothing new. It's the same old thing we've been struggling with for years. When we're saved, our "old man" dies, but he constantly struggles to rise again and take control of our lives.

Unfortunately, hell knows exactly what your particular weaknesses are. That's where you'll be tested over and over again, and you'll be tested in ways that others can only imagine. Because others might never think of succumbing to that particular temptation, Satan doesn't even bother tempting them in that way.

This word *beset,* according to *Strong's,* is what happens to a competitor getting ready for a race when someone or something suddenly distracts him in his surroundings. As a consequence, what he sees hinders him from concentrating on the task at hand—his important race. That can be fatal, and it happens very easily.

The presence of any weight in your life changes your focus. Instead of focusing on God, you begin to focus on the things and the people around you. Thus, any weight becomes a hindrance. It could cause you to be sidelined from the race, to fall behind, or even to be forcibly removed from the race.

When a serious runner is standing on his mark at a starting line, he knows that it's not the time to be looking around. He has one thing on his mind. He has a race to run. Anything that he allows to distract him will only hinder his prospects for victory. With those who are not as serious, such distractions can easily occur.

When people are newly saved, they have a joy that seems to know no bounds. They can hardly talk without tears coming to their eyes. They love to read the Word of God and listen to good teaching—wherever they can find it. They love to go to church, and those moments in which they can interact with other Christians brings great joy to their lives.

But soon the weights begin to come, and they start dreading to go to church and meeting other Christians. Instead of bringing them joy, it now becomes a chore for them. They say a prayer now and then to ease their conscience, but they dread the idea of a real prayer time. No wonder their old habits begin to surface!

Where are you in the race that the Lord has set before you? Are you diligent in your pursuit of God, steadfast in your commitment to expanding His kingdom, and faithful in supporting His servants? Above all, are you giving of your heart in prayer on behalf of all His saints?

When a Christian shuns fellowship with other Christians, the devil smiles. When he stops studying the Bible, the devil laughs. When he stops praying, the devil shouts for joy.

Corrie Ten Boom

FIFTY-EIGHT

When Desire Stagnates

And it shall come to pass, that every thing that liveth, which moveth, whithersoever the rivers shall come, shall live.

Ezekiel 47:9

The prophet Ezekiel had a vision of a place that badly needed watering, and then he saw rivers flowing toward it. That's a picture of the abundant life the Lord offers us. But not every place benefited. Ezekiel went on to say:

But the miry places thereof and the marshes thereof shall not be healed.

Ezekiel 47:11

This is phenomenal! The vision Ezekiel received that day depicts great revival, the flowing of rivers of life into a dry situation, and the bringing of new and abundant life to everything it touched. But, for some reason, some places were left untouched by it all. Why would that be?

"Miry places" and "marshes" are places that already have some water, but that water is not fresh. It gets trapped in there, and then it stagnates. Right there in the midst of the flow of the river of God, there are untouched and unchanged places. While everyone around them is being changed, they remain much as they were before.

Swampy, or miry places represent self-centeredness, an inward focus. Water comes in, but then it's trapped and, because it has no outlet, it stagnates.

Some people are like that. They're so self-centered, so inwardly focused, that nothing else matters to them. They demand that others let them have and do what they want. And as difficult as it seems, as God is moving around them, they remain unmoved by it. Other people are being healed on every side of them, and yet they remain crippled and in need. Nothing seems to reach them. Heaven can be declared in such a sweet way that others almost feel as if they're already there. Yet these people remain unmoved. How terrible!

David knew what it was to be trapped in "miry clay," but he came forth:

He brought me up also out of an horrible pit, out of the miry clay, and set my feet upon a rock, and established my goings.

Psalm 40:2

Let God bring you out today and then get quickly into the flow of His river. **Refuse to stay in your swamp any longer.**

Thank you, Lord, for showing me where the miry places are in my life. Like You did for Your servant David, set my foot on a rock and establish my goings. Help me not to be so self-absorbed that I'm unable to be renewed by the waters of Your Spirit.

If there be anything that is capable of setting the soul in a large place it is absolute abandonment to God. It diffuses in the soul a peace that flows like a river and the righteousness which is as the waves of the sea.

François Fénelon

FIFTY-NINE

The Tragedy of Disobedience

And it came to pass by the way in the inn, that the Lord met him and sought to kill him.

Exodus 4:24

The tragedy of allowing sin into your life is graphically illustrated in the life of Moses. This man Moses was such a great man that only God occupies more space in the Bible than him. He was a man who stood on holy ground and talked to God face-to-face. He witnessed his rod turned into a serpent. He learned the name of God when the Lord said to him, "I Am that I Am." Still, there was sin in Moses' life.

Moses had just gotten to the Holiday Inn, had checked in, signing his VISA slip in the process, and had gone to his room and taken off his shoes so that he could relax a little, when the Lord appeared and tried to kill him. And, again, we're talking about one of the greatest men in the Bible.

What does all of this mean? It means that you will never reach a place in God that you can afford to overlook sin. **You will never become so popular, so powerful, so useful, and so necessary that God will overlook your sin.**

Most Bible scholars believe that when God met Moses that day and tried to kill him it was because he had not circumcised his second son. His wife, Zipporah, was offended by the fact that God told the people to circumcise their children, so she opposed Moses in this matter, and he gave in to her. Satan whispered into his ear: "Why not let her have her way this time? What will it hurt? You have a great mandate from God to deliver the people, and you don't need to be distracted by something as minor as this. Believe me, God will understand."

But in God's eyes, this was no small thing. Circumcision was part of a covenant God had made with Abraham and his descendants. The physical act of circumcision was a sign of separation between the followers of Jehovah and others, and Moses, as one of the major leaders of His people, could not be exempt. He needed to get his own house in order if he was to lead others. After all, God didn't need Moses. *He* was the deliverer!

Have you ever slipped into feelings of entitlement? Are there little areas in your life that have been compromised as a result of the enemy whispering in your ear? What do you think might have been the cost to your own destiny, and perhaps that of another, because of your lack of obedience? What are some small things you can do today to turn that around?

A Christian should always remember that the value of his good works is not based on their number and excellence, but on the love of God which prompts him to do these things.

John of the Cross

SIXTY

Called to a Sacred Desire

The wages of sin is death; but the gift of God is eternal life through Jesus Christ our Lord.

Romans 6:23

It's true that God is loving, patient, and longsuffering, but there comes a time when His grace can no longer hold back the results of your sin. Before that time comes, He does everything He can to help you get your act together. But eventually He will have to step aside and allow the consequences of sin to take over.

In our pride, we often try to gloss over our wrongdoings. Pride brings nothing but self-seeking and self-promoting. It fills men and women with ego, conceit, arrogance, jealousy, gossip, lying, and prejudice. Set aside your pride and deal with the sin that is in your life before it destroys you.

How can we read the Bible and not understand the consequences of sin? Consider, for instance, Adam and Eve—their disobedience cost them Paradise. Consider King Saul—he lost his throne. Consider Samson—he died a prisoner of the enemy. Consider Aaron's two sons; they were judged by God and burned up by His fire. Consider Eli and his two sons—they died in quick succession for their folly. Consider the people of the tribe of Korah—the ground opened up under them and swallowed them up alive. Consider the three thousand people who would not obey Moses in the wilderness—they were all destroyed. And the list goes on and on. It contains kings, priests, and prophets. **You can't take the risk of living a life void of spiritual desire**, a life given over to the lust of the flesh.

When sin has been removed, then restoration can take place. Anytime we locate some sin, any sin, in our life, we need to get it out. It may be pride, lust, gossip, or bitterness. But, whatever it is, we need to identify it and get it out of there. Then allow the Holy Ghost to fumigate that place and refill us with His Spirit.

It's time to lay aside every weight and the sin which does so easily beset us, and to run with patience the race that is set before us. Leave no pagan altars standing. Tear them all down. Get rid of them once and for all. If you give the devil any space at all, he'll attempt to rule your life again. Show God the intensity of your spiritual desire, and He will reward you handsomely.

If we want the Word of God to have authority in our life, there is only one way–obey it. If we want the Holy Spirit to have authority in our life, there is only one way–Obey Him. If we always obey impulses of fear or doubt or resentment, what will have authority over our minds? Fear and doubt and resentment.

Tom Marshall

SIXTY-ONE

Obedience: The Fruit of Spiritual Desire

Now go and smite Amalek, and utterly destroy all that they have, and spare them not; but slay both man and woman, infant and suckling, ox and sheep, camel and ass....

But Saul and the people spared Agag, and the best of the sheep, and of the oxen, and of the fatlings, and the lambs, and all that was good, and would not utterly destroy them: but every thing that was vile and refuse, that they destroyed utterly.

1 Samuel 15:3,9

In God's Word, from Genesis to Revelation, obedience is the key to everything, but that obedience is possible only to those who are possessors of spiritual desire.

The biblical account of the early history of man begins with Adam's disobedience and moves on to Abraham's obedience. It contrasts Moses' disobedience with Joshua's obedience, Eli's disobedience with Samuel's obedience, and Saul's disobedience with David's obedience. That's just the beginning of the list, and it was all written as an example for us. In every chapter of His Word, God is trying to show us that it pays to obey Him, and it doesn't pay to disobey Him.

There is even an element of obedience necessary to our salvation. God said that we must believe with our hearts and confess with our mouths, and we have to do that to be saved. He has promised to send His Spirit upon those who obey Him:

> *And we are his witnesses of these things; and so is also the Holy Ghost, whom God hath given to them that obey him.*
>
> Acts 5:32

Faith is revealed through obedience, for it is nothing more than obeying what God has said because we believe it. If we don't obey, it means that we don't really believe.

Throughout Paul's writings to the church, there are interspersed instructions to be obeyed, and the New Testament concludes with the powerful book of Revelation that declares:

> *Blessed is he that readeth, and they that hear the words of this prophecy, and keep those things which are written therein.*
>
> Revelation 1:3

> *Blessed is he that keepeth the sayings of the prophecy of this book.*
>
> Revelation 22:7

> *Blessed are they that do his commandments, that they may have right to the tree of life, and may enter in through the gates into the city.*
>
> Revelation 22:14

So from the beginning of the Bible to the end, all of God's promised blessings hinge upon our obedience to Him and His teachings, and **our obedience to Him hinges upon maintaining our spiritual desire**.

Lord, help to desire more of You, Your Presence, Your sweet fellowship—give me a deeper revelation of Your Will in every situation. Help me to partake of Your Divine Nature.

The man that believes will obey; failure to obey is convincing proof that there is no true faith present. To attempt the impossible God must give faith or there will be none, and He gives faith to the obedient heart only.

A.W. Tozer

SIXTY-TWO

Favor Requires Obedience

Samuel also said unto Saul, The Lord sent me to anoint thee to be king over his people, over Israel: now therefore hearken thou unto the voice of the words of the Lord.

1 Samuel 15:1

The prophet Samuel recorded the entire story of this man Saul who became Israel's first king. He started out on the right track. He was anointed by God and could prophesy under God's power. But then, in time, disobedience came into his life. With that disobedience, came jealousy. Next, the jealousy turned to rage. The result was that the end of Saul, who had started out so well, was very sad. At the beginning of this fifteenth chapter, as Samuel was preparing to convey to Saul God's instructions, he reminded Saul of how he had risen to such heights of power.

When God's favor is upon us that brings strong obligations on our part. He doesn't give us His power just to use as we want. The more we have from Him, the more important it is to be obedient to Him in all things. God now had a job for Saul to do, and He had a reason for telling him what he was about to tell him. God is God, and He doesn't have to state His reasons for telling us to do something, but in this case He graciously did:

> *Thus saith the Lord of hosts, I remember that which Amalek did to Israel, how he laid wait for him in the way, when he came up from Egypt.*
>
> 1 Samuel 15:2

The Amalekites had not wanted to allow the children of Israel to pass through their land, and they had tried to hire a prophet named Balaam to curse God's chosen ones. This was the reason for God's severity toward them, and who was Saul to question it?

The sad thing is that when Saul returned from his mission, he reported to Samuel that he had done all that God required of him. This, of course, was not true, and God had already told Samuel that He was sorry He had made Saul king. Saul was bold enough in his disobedience to think that he could fool the prophet, but Samuel now asked the haughty king:

> *What meaneth then this bleating of the sheep in mine ears, and the lowing of the oxen which I hear?*
>
> 1 Samuel 15:14

God wasn't fooled and neither was Samuel, and he let that be known. Even a king cannot disobey God and be free of consequences.

Father God, You alone are worthy of my complete obedience. Search my heart and shine Your light on any hidden place where I have disregarded Your Word.

There's some task which the God of all the universe, the great Creator, your redeemer in Jesus Christ has for you to do, and which will remain undone and incomplete until by faith and obedience you step into the will of God.

Alan Redpath

SIXTY-THREE

Good Desire vs. Godly Desire

Love not the world, neither the things that are in the world. If any man love the world, the love of the Father is not in him.

1 John 2:15

Saul had always loved the Lord in some capacity. He had never completely abandoned his faith in God. But the desires of his flesh had been allowed to take precedence over the will of God, and that could not stand. Then, in pride, he did not want to give up his profession, but the reality of his life testified against him. **The love of the world and the love of the Lord don't mix.**

Saul was the king, but that didn't matter. Clearly it's not enough to have been saved for years or to have done great things for God's kingdom. He demands obedience today of each and every one of us if we're to claim Him as Lord of our lives. Saul was quick to blame others and, thus, to excuse his own participation in the wrongdoing. "So-and-So did it" or "So-and-So made me do it" have been common justifications since the beginning of time. They haven't worked until now, and they won't work in the future.

Next, Saul tried two more excuses: that he had done most of what the Lord had commanded and that what he had not done was because he had a better plan. Saul had obeyed in part, and in what part he had not obeyed, his intention had been good. He wanted to use those sheep and oxen to make a sacrifice to God. What could possibly be wrong with that?

Samuel's answer to this good-sounding excuse is revealing. He reminded Saul again that when he had been little in his own sight, God had raised him up. Then, when he had been exalted and made king, God had given him a very explicit order. It could not have been misunderstood, and yet Saul had not obeyed it. Samuel refused to accept what Saul had done as being good in any way. Rather, he described it as "*evil in the sight of the LORD.*"

Amazingly, Saul continued to assert his innocence, and he repeated the whole story. He had done exactly what the Lord had told him, but the people had insisted on keeping certain animals to sacrifice to God. To this, Samuel responded with words that have rung out down through the centuries:

> *Behold, to obey is better than sacrifice, and to hearken than the fat of rams.*
>
> 1 Samuel 15:22

Nothing can replace obedience. Nothing!

Thank You Lord for Your Spirit at work in me causing me to will and to do your good pleasure. Help me to trust You in all things and to be quick to obey You at all times. Amen!

God is God. Because He is God, He is worthy of my trust and obedience. I will find rest nowhere but in His holy will, a will that is unspeakably beyond my largest notions of what He is up to.

Elisabeth Elliot

SIXTY-FOUR

Desire Demonstrates Faithfulness

Hath the Lord as great delight in burnt offerings and sacrifices, as in obeying the voice of the Lord? Behold, to obey is better than sacrifice, and to hearken than the fat of rams.

1 Samuel 15:22

The context of this verse is very interesting. The sacrifices of the Old Testament were an integral part of the worship to God. So it is showing us that God doesn't welcome our worship if and when we're not willing to be obedient to Him. Samuel went on to make his point even more forcefully:

For rebellion is as the sin of witchcraft, and stubbornness is as iniquity and idolatry.

1 Samuel 15:23

When Saul placed his will in direct competition to God's will and insisted again and again that he had done the right thing, he entered into open rebellion against the Almighty. It's one thing to make a mistake, but it's something else entirely to directly and intentionally disobey God, flaunt it, and think that we can get away with it. **Do we dare enter into competition with the God of the universe?**

Witchcraft! Rebellion! Idolatry! Was Samuel using words that were much too strong? Not at all. This was a serious sin, and the consequences Samuel was about to announce would show just how serious a sin it really was in God's sight:

> *Because thou hast rejected the word of the Lord, he hath also rejected thee from being king.*
>
> 1 Samuel 15:23

The attitude of so many today is: "I don't care what you show me in the Bible. I know what I want, and I know what I believe, and I'm sure that God understands." Well, you'd better care, because the consequences of direct disobedience to God are serious for anyone.

Sometimes we need to stop and take a long, close look at our lives. We need to examine every area, not just the overall, general direction of our lives, but the little areas where we might be falling short. It's usually in neglecting the small things that we are kept from fulfilling the big things God has prepared for us. What are some of the little areas of your life that might need "realigning" to God's Holy Word?

Rest in this–it is His business to lead, command, impel, send, call, or whatever you want to call it. It is your business to obey, follow, move, respond, or what have you . . . The sound of "gentle stillness" after all the thunder and wind have passed will be the ultimate Word from God.

Jim Elliot

SIXTY-FIVE

Truth and Desire

Pride goeth before destruction, and an haughty spirit before a fall.

Proverbs 16:18

To most of us, idolatry is the overt act of bowing the knee before some graven image, some other god. But, in reality, it's much more than that. If we imagine certain things about God and then act like they're so, that's as much idolatry as the overt act of bowing the knee to false gods. He has given us His Word, and it tells us everything He wants us to know about Him. To make Him anything other than what the Bible says He is, is the worst kind of sin one could possibly commit.

As children of God, we all know that periodically God deals with us about things in our lives that are not pleasing to Him. If we fail to quickly and willingly rid ourselves of these obstacles to His love, this says to Him that we assume that

He's going to allow us to get by with whatever we're doing that He's not happy with. That's the kind of pride that goes before destruction and a fall.

Even though it may seem you're getting along just fine, there will come a moment in which the Holy Spirit will step aside and allow judgment to flood in upon you. "I've done all that I can do," He'll have to say. "I have wooed you and convicted you. I tried to get your conscience to set off alarm bells inside of you. I tried everything I knew to try, but you haven't heeded." Then the Holy Ghost has to withdraw His presence and allow you to become fair game for the devil.

In His mercy, God may delay judgment, hoping we will wake up and smell the coffee, but too often we instead think we have gotten away with it. But the longer His judgment is delayed, the more severe the punishment will be when it does come. Just because we're not immediately executed doesn't mean that we're safe from punishment. God's judgment of sin is sure.

If your love for God has grown cold, let His Spirit renew you today.

Father God, help me to see You as You really are—to be circumspect and sober-minded. Teach me what it means to fear, respect, and reverence You. I desire to know You in Truth and to walk in the light of that Truth. Help me to gird up the loins of my mind and to pursue Your Holiness with singleness of heart. Amen.

Scripture is clear that it is important to know the Father through His Word, and if we want to be a part of what the Father is doing and to be able to see where He is moving then it is clear that we must obey His commands. It is important to be biblically literate, but we must also be biblically obedient!

John Wimber

SIXTY-SIX

Uncompromising Desire

And be renewed in the spirit of your mind ...that ye put on the new man, which after God is created in righteousness and true holiness.

Ephesians 4:23,24

There's a pattern to be found throughout the Bible that seems to be repeated all too often in modern life. A prophet (maybe a pastor in modern terms) comes our way and preaches the Word of God. We're "turned on" by it, and our hearts are stirred so that we make a public commitment to forsake sin and serve God.

I've watched it happen thousands of times in altars across the world. "God, I'm going to straighten my life out and get my act together. I'll forsake every sin, and I'll start doing something meaningful for You. You can depend on me, Lord. Use me."

But strangely, within a very short time, many of those who have uttered such sincere-sounding pledges have forgotten their words of commitment. What has happened? I'm convinced that **people** are sincere when they pray, but they **make a fatal mistake in not allowing total change to come to their lives.** Those sacred moments at the altar turn out to be just a little prayer that was prayed with no meaningful follow-up, and no real lasting commitment.

As we see in the Old Testament, every time a new leader came to the throne in Israel, he would call for a cleansing of the temple. He would call for the high places dedicated to idols to be torn down, and then he would bring back the worship of the true God.

In these moments, all of Israel would rejoice. They had come back to God, and He had come back to them. But invariably they left a few of the high places standing, and this resulted in a diluted faith, a partial obedience, and eventual backsliding.

The devil doesn't need much room to insert a wedge into your life. God's Word advises us: *"Neither give place to the devil"* (Ephesians 4:27). We're not to give him a place, because when he has found even a small place, he works tirelessly to enlarge it. If you leave a little bit of temper, a little bit of bitterness, or a little bit of unforgiveness, that's all he needs in order to slowly take control of you.

Being moved by the Spirit of God is not wrong. That's a good beginning. Making a commitment to God is not wrong. We all need to do it. But these must be followed by meaningful changes in our everyday life so that we can truly become soldiers of the cross.

If you do not plan to live the Christian life totally committed to knowing your God and to walking in obedience to Him, then don't begin, for this is what Christianity is all about. It is a change of citizenship, a change of governments, a change of allegiance. If you have no intention of letting Christ rule your life, then forget Christianity; it is not for you.

Kay Arthur

SIXTY-SEVEN

Desire Nothing but Christ

For I say, through the grace given unto me, to every man that is among you, not to think of himself more highly than he ought to think; but to think soberly, according as God hath dealt to every man the measure of faith.

Romans 12:3

At home I have a painting that I love. It's of a small girl. She has on her mother's dress and her father's shoes, and she's trying to hold up the dress so that she can walk in those big shoes. Every morning and every night that I'm home, I get down on my knees beside that painting, and I say, "God, that's me. That's how I feel with Your mantle on me. Help me never to lose that sense of awe at my smallness and Your greatness." That's exactly what happened to Saul. As long as he was small in his own eyes, he was fine. But just as soon as he decided that he somehow deserved to be king, then God had to bring him down.

Pride and lust are two forces that have caused many believers to miss God's best. These are the besetting sins of our day. Pride is thinking more highly of yourself than you should—it thirsts after honor and the applause of men.

Lust, in one form or another, seems to be the besetting sin for most people of our age. More people are destroyed by it than by any other temptation. "Lust of the flesh" is craving fleshly desires and pleasures, while "lust of the eye" is covetousness—wanting something that doesn't belong to you.

It seems to be an obsession of our generation to work hard and accumulate as much as possible in life, almost as if there were some prize for the person who has left behind the most toys. Life is short, we rationalize, and so we need to experience as much of it as possible as quickly as possible.

But life is not a contest, and things are not the treasures we should be seeking. Yet if we seek first the Kingdom of God and His righteousness, these things are promised us. Remembering who we were without Christ should cure us of lusting after the things of this world. Certainly, we can be sure that **falling in love with Jesus will cure all pride.**

Lord, help me to recognize where I am falling short. Help me to see that you are the force behind all of my success and the reason why I have peace and joy in my life today. It is Your love, and Your righteousness working in me that causes me to triumph.

No mortal man or devil can supersede the will of God for your life. If you lay hold of this truth, it will set you free. But there is only one person who can get you out of the will of God and that person is you.

John Bevere

SIXTY-EIGHT

A Purifying Desire

Seeing ye have purified your souls in obeying the truth through the Spirit unto unfeigned love of the brethren.

1 Peter 1:22

Evan Roberts, the great Welsh revivalist, left us a powerful testimony about how revival begins. Today we consider that the most important elements of revival are great advertising and great organization. But, although "Come and get your miracle," and "Come and see the man of God who will bring you healing!" may be interesting slogans, they could never produce revival. There may indeed be miracles, and people may be saved and blessed, but true revival always starts with a small group of people who have purified themselves.

After he had fasted and prayed for many days, Evan Roberts went to church one night with a message from God. The crowd that night consisted of just seventeen people, and the message he had for them consisted of four things that they should do: (1) they should confess all known sin, (2) search out all secret and doubtful things, (3) be ready to obey the Holy Spirit instantly, and (4) confess the Lord Jesus openly.

This was God's recipe for revival, and the people accepted it. Within the first twenty-four hours, more than thirty thousand people had been touched by the revival, and within a short time, the whole world had to sit up and take notice of what God was doing in Wales.

What's wrong with us today? Why doesn't revival come? Personally, I'm convinced that it's because we have some miry places in our lives. There are some things that we need to get rid of. And we all need to start obeying the Word of God. Disobedience to God might not always kill you outrightly, but it will surely contaminate your soul and prevent you from going deeper in God.

Revival is not just getting happy, shaking, quaking, and falling on the floor. That may be part of it, but that alone is not enough. **True revival will touch every part of your community**. It will send you outside the church walls with a message about what's happening in your life. And many others will be blessed as a result.

It's time to confess and forsake anything that hinders and to make it right. Stir up the miry places. Cause the stagnant waters to come forth and get those parts of your life into the river so that you can be healed. Say to God today, "Whatever it takes, let my will be broken, so that I can be one with You." In short, let Him renew your first love and cause to flame again the ebbing embers of your soul.

Some people do not like to hear much of repentance; but I think it is so necessary that if I should die in the pulpit, I would desire to die preaching repentance, and if out of the pulpit I would desire to die practicing it.

Matthew Henry

SIXTY-NINE

Intense Desire Praises Intensely

Praise him for his mighty acts: praise him according to his excellent greatness.

Psalm 150:2

Desire determines the intensity of your worship to God, just as it does the intensity of your relationship to any other person. That's why God is waiting to hear your praise.

His Word admonishes us to praise Him for His mighty acts, to praise Him according to His excellent greatness. He knows it all, but He wants to hear you say it. He wants to hear your words of love.

"Tell Me," He's saying. "Let Me hear it. Praise Me for delivering Daniel from the lion's den. Praise Me for what I did for the three Hebrew boys in the fiery furnace. Praise Me for what happened at the Red Sea. Tell Me. I want to hear your voice of praise."

Each of us likes to be praised, and that's because we were made in God's image. **We were created to** *"show forth the praises of the Lord"*:

> *But ye are a chosen generation, a royal priesthood, an holy nation, a peculiar people; that ye should show forth the praises of him who hath called you out of darkness into his marvelous light.*
>
> 1 Peter 2:9

We all know what it feels like to have someone bragging on us. A great smile comes over our face, we throw back our shoulders, and we're ready to take on a lion. That's how David felt the day he said:

> *For by thee I have run through a troop: by my God have I leaped over a wall.*
>
> 2 Samuel 22:30

Praise, more than anything else, will turn your life around and set you on a path toward victory.

God knows that He's good, but He wants to hear you say it anyway. He's no egomaniac, but He has chosen to dwell in the praises of His people.

If you learn to come to God in this way, you will be welcomed inside His most intimate sanctuary every time. He wants to grant you access to His throne room, to give you the very keys to His kingdom. Your praise speaks to Him of your love, and your love will unlock to you all of the treasures of heaven.

Praise is the highest form of prayer. In all things, at all times, praise the Lord! Psalm 150:6 proclaims that every thing that has breath should praise the Lord. Author John Piper sums it up this way: "All of history is moving toward one great goal, the white-hot worship of God and his Son among all the peoples of the earth." Are you part of the movement?

In worship, our hunger for God is both satisfied and increased. In His Presence, we desire "all the fullness of God" and we want to be done with sin, we want the church purified, and we long for the return of Christ. We are even homesick for heaven.

Erwin Lutzer

SEVENTY

The Secret of Divine Desire

Enter into his gates with thanksgiving, and into his courts with praise: be thankful unto him, and bless his name.

Psalm 100:4

If you want to meet with God, you have to come to Him through gates of thanksgiving. That's where He lives. You cannot come to Him without passing through courts of praise.

Lawrence and I decided to put a combination lock on our back door, and we gave the combination to a few people we were close to, people we knew we could trust. Do you realize that God has given you the combination to His door? Thanksgiving, praise, and worship—these are the keys that give you access to God at any time and anywhere. Wow! That's powerful!

God not only longs for your expressions of love to Him; He makes it mutual. He whispers words of love back into your heart too. **The Lord always makes known to you how very much He loves you**, and then He's waiting to hear that you appreciate Him too.

In true prayer, you think of His goodness and what He's done for you, and your heart wants to leap out of you for the joy of it all. You think about where you used to be and where you could be, and you want to thank Him for where you are today.

The devil doesn't want you to think about those things, and he does all within his power to keep your mind cluttered and confused. Rather than think about where you used to be and where you might have been, he wants to make you dissatisfied with where you are today. He wants to keep you focused on your current problems and how you're going to get out of them, so that you'll forget that if God did it once, then He can do it again.

The devil doesn't want you to start praising God. He knows that if you start praising Him, you'll unlock the windows of heaven over your life, and God will look down from heaven and say, "What do you need from Me today, My child? Just name it, and it's yours."

Tell the Lord today what He's worth to you, how much you love Him and how good He has been to You! Be mindful of His goodness and mercy, praise Him continually—give thanks always for all things! Don't let the enemy rob you of the fullness of joy to be found in Christ! Don't let him keep you from pursuing your heart's deepest desire—to praise and worship Your Lord with all your heart, mind and strength. There's power in your praises—and that power is God Himself.

The one concern of the devil is to keep Christians from praying. He fears nothing from prayerless studies, prayerless work, and prayerless religion. He laughs at our toil, mocks at our wisdom, but trembles when we pray.

Samuel Chadwick